Black Diamond

BLACKDIAMONDEQUIPMENT.COM

AN ICE CLIMBER'S GUIDE TO MICHIGAN'S
UPPER PENINSULA

Copyright © 2019 Old Bull Publishing

All rights reserved. No part of this publication may be reproduced, distributed, or transmitted in any form or by any means, including photocopying, recording, or other electronic or mechanical methods, without the prior written permission of the publisher. For permission requests, write to the publisher, addressed "Attention: Permissions Coordinator," at the address below.

Printed in the United States of America
by Four Colour Print Group, Louisville, Kentucky.

ISBN 978-0-578-41589-5

Old Bull Publishing
514 N Third St.
Marquette MI, 49855

Ordering Information:
To order this book please contact Down Wind Sports.
(906) 226-7112
www.downwindsports.com

Cover: Bulls On Parade
X Angela Vanwiemeersch
📷 Keith Ladzinski

Title: Mosquito Beach
X Brett Merlin
📷 Mike Wilkinson

Foreword by Conrad Anker	2
Welcome To The U.P.	4
Local Beta	6
History	8
Geology	12
Ecology	13
Rules, Regulations, and Ethics	14
Michigan Ice Fest	16
Ice Beta: How to Use This Guide	18
Ice Grading	20
Using the Maps, Disclaimer	21
Pictured Rocks and Grand Island	
Introduction to the Area	22
Things to Know	24
Front Country	26
Lakeshore Trail	36
Miner's Beach to Mosquito Beach	58
Mosquito Beach to Chapel Beach	64
East of Chapel Beach	78
Inland	86
Grand Island East Chanel	92
Grand Island Trout Bay	100
Grand Island West Shore	110
Grand Island North Shore	126
Rock River Canyon	
Introduction to the Area	134
Climbs	136
Marquette County	
Introduction to the Area	138
Climbs	140
Copper Country	
Introduction to the Area	148
Climbs	150
Western Upper Peninsula	
Introduction to the Area	154
Climbs	156
Route Index and Tick List	170
Routes by Grade	178
Photographers	186
Special Thanks	187
The Authors	188
Notes	190
Sisu Shot	197

Contents

Tiger Country
Jesse Huey ✕
Jason Gebauer

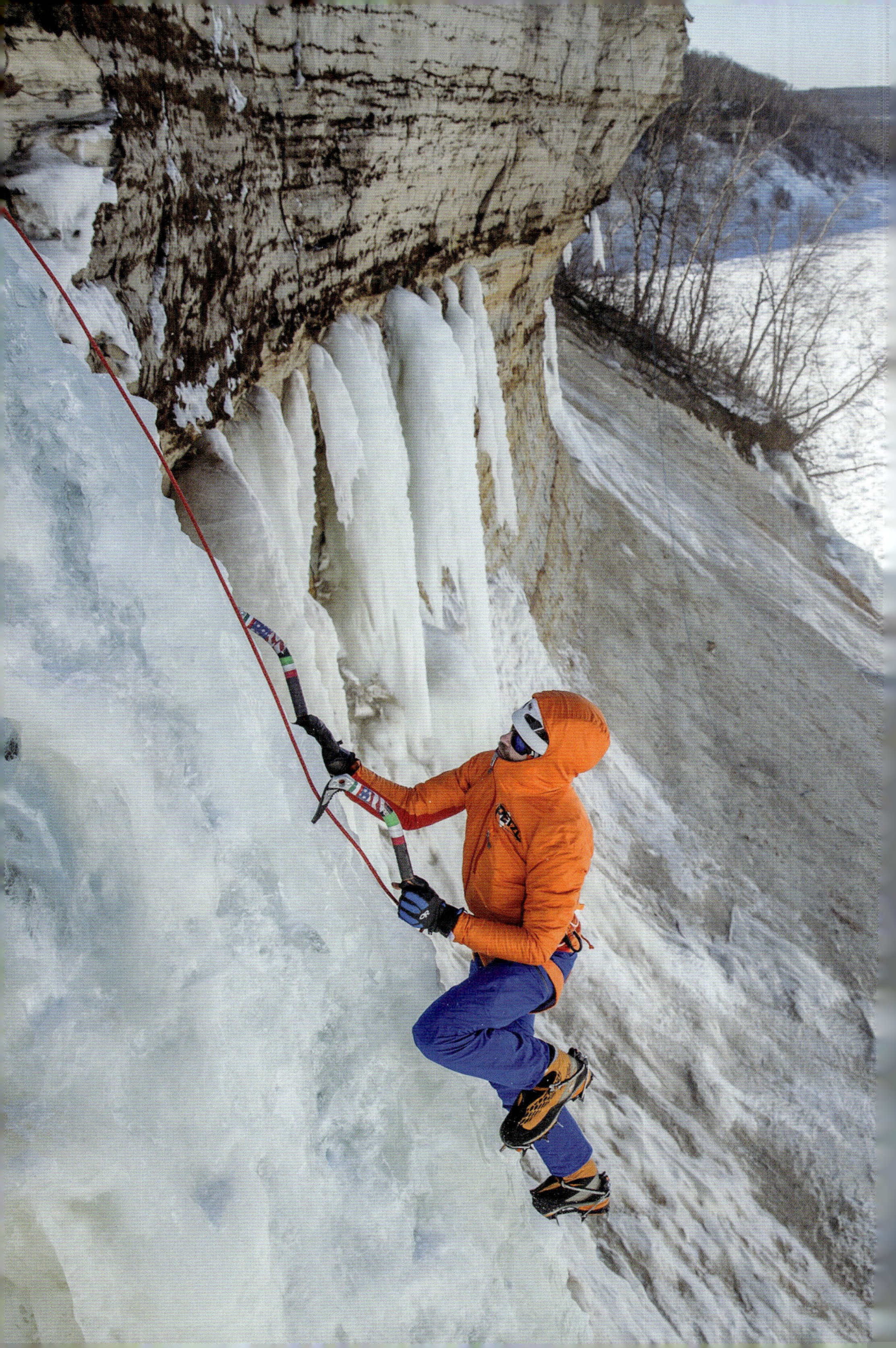

There is an adventure waiting out there just for you. All you have to do is find it, and we can help. With decades of experiece climbing in the Upper Peninsula we know this place better than anyone. Specializing in climbing adventures for all experience levels and all interest, the Michigan Ice Fest Guides can help you find your perfect adventure. Learn more at IceClimbMichigan.com

Unrivaled Local Knowledge.
Unrivaled Experience.
Unrivaled Fun.

We are the plain stubborn.

Everything we make is designed by climbers, for climbers. Each piece is crafted by peak and crag to give you absolute protection, comfort and mobility when you really need it.

Rab®
THE MOUNTAIN PEOPLE

WWW.RAB.EQUIPMENT

WE HAVE THE GEAR TO GET YOU THERE!

DOWN WIND SPORTS

The Upper Peninsula's Most Complete Outfitter

Aaron Peterson

www.DownWindSports.com @downwindsports

FOREWORD

Winter in the northern hardwoods has a character-defining silence. The dormant trees and subtle contours have a very primal and refreshing feel. When winter is in full grip the cold tames Lake Superior, locking waves and currents under a blanket of ice. Pictured Rocks National Lakeshore is a combination of forest and lake that exemplifies this winter wonderland. While for some this is misery, for ice climbers, this is just the right mix for adventure.

Along one section of the southern Lake Superior shore a 500-million-year-old belt of sandstone is exposed to the lake. These 50-200 foot cliffs, combined with the forest hydrology, have created seeps that have painted the rock with brown, orange, blue and white mineral stains. The same minerals that color the rock also permeate the ice, leading to uniquely colored pillars, smears and flows. This unique combination of lake, cliff and forest in winter is of great interest to ice climbers.

Navigating the forest, in the calm of dawn, to find a flow of ice is an adventurous way to start the day. The hike warms you up, you look around the forest and try to decipher if you're at the right climb. Once you rap in and pull your ropes a sense of commitment settles in. If the lake is frozen it's a tricky walk out. If the lake is open there is an ominous weight of, "We have to do this. The only way out is up." This combination of dense forest and expansive singularity of the lake create a unique place to be!

Setting expectations based on comparisons is a sure way to leave you wanting. If one embraces the beauty of the location, accepting it for what it is, the journey to the climb becomes as significant as the ascent. From the squeak of cold dry snow to the vertical bushwhacking, there are situations that will challenge your backcountry skills. Due to the composition of the soft sandstone, the ever-evolving art of drytooling has thankfully not caught on at Pictured Rocks. Come to Pictured Rocks for the ice and you'll be pleasantly surprised. Dairyland, the classic pillar of bovine proportions, and HMR, a sustained sheet of rust-colored ice, are the iconic representation of Michigan ice. They are deservedly on every ice climber's bucket list.

The ice and forest will leave you with a happy sense of exhaustion, one that is replenished in Munising, the local community partnered with Pictured Rocks National Lakeshore. The denizens of Michigan's Upper Peninsula, the UP, refer to themselves as Yoopers and it's their hospitality that makes a trip to Pictured Rocks worth it. The town offers a range of bivy options, from warm and pampered, to the stoic and cold. Nourishment? The cold spurs an appetite for salty, rich foods. The local restaurants can satiate your need for fried food. Taking time to catch up with the host community is pretty cool. Ice climbers and local citizens share the value of perseverance and with this common bond are welcoming of the climbing tribe.

Climbing is defined by the interaction we have with our fellow humans. The skills to belay are the international sign language of our community. Within this language there are dialects and Michigan Ice is welcoming and warm. It's powerful energy. Harness this mindset to venture out into a cold and unforgiving environment. Find your vertical adventure in the Upper Peninsula. May you dream of steep cold climbs along the Lake Superior shore past, present and future.

Safe climbing,

Conrad Anker

East Channel Curtains
Conrad Anker
Max Lowe

WELCOME TO THE U.P., EH!

When people think of culture they often picture things like opera houses and art galleries. We like that stuff too, but we have a slightly different version of culture here. Music comes from the winds howling off of the largest lake in the world, or the lyrical murmur of water flowing down a creek. Pictures are painted on the rocks by eons of rich minerals flowing through the ground and galleries of ancient trees paint the forest with colors no brush could rival. The stark beauty of winter isn't just a season here, it's a part of us.

It's wild out there, and as climbers we wouldn't have it any other way. Ice and snow decorate the land more often than not. We embrace and revel in what others think of as a bleak time, one to be waited out and wished away. Our passion for ice climbing stems from this wild culture and is fueled by the allure of the cold and snow.

The U.P. offers some of the country's most unique and interesting ice climbing. Many climbs rise magnificently up and out of Lake Superior. Expansive views stretch out over the lake to an uninterrupted horizon, giving climbers rare glimpses of exposure seldom found in the Midwest.

Some years Superior freezes into an eery moonscape. Other years it does not, and can be a temperamental and often violent climbing partner. Thunderous, crashing waves driven by hurricane force winds take their turn pounding the ancient bedrock and the bases of many of the climbs. The climber, gripped to the max as the vibrations of the waves slamming the shore pulse through the ice, struggles upward through frigid air while heavy snow falls silently around them. It's an experience akin to the most soulful music and can affect the spirit like the very best art.

This wilder version of culture permeates the landscape and has extended itself to the fine people who live here. Walk into any coffee shop or bar in the Upper Peninsula and you'll be greeted by warm smiles despite the bitter cold. A few drinks and you're welcomed into the fold. A few good stories and you're family. The stress and efforts of the day die away as strangers become friends and stories become legends.

So welcome to the U.P., eh! It's wild. It's friendly. It's not like anywhere else, and we think you'll enjoy it UP here!

Heading North to the Promised Land
Mike Wilkinson

LOCAL BETA

GETTING THERE
Let's be honest, the U.P. is a long way from anywhere. Add a good dose of winter and your travel plans can, and may, turn a bit spicy. The cities of Munising, Marquette and Houghton act as hubs for ice climbing in the Upper Peninsula. All three are full service towns, with all of the amenities you could need, albeit in a slightly more rustic manner in some cases.

Marquette, the largest city in the Upper Peninsula, is centrally located and provides the most varied and modern service. As the "Queen City" of the U.P. you can get everything you need and more here.

Munising is 44 miles east of Marquette and is home to the vast majority of the climbing. It's a small town and many businesses close during the winter season, so be prepared.

Houghton is 100 miles west of Marquette in the Keweenaw Peninsula. Known for its deep snow and small town feel, Houghton makes a good base for climbs in the Copper Country and Western U.P.

Each city offers a distinct culture with plenty of lodging, restaurant, bar and micro-brewery options.

DRIVING
The most dangerous activity you will encounter on your climbing trip will be driving to the U.P. in the winter! During the long winter season, major snow events and sub-zero temperatures are common. Snowfall totals from storms are often measured in feet, not inches, and lake effect storms along Lake Superior are common. But, as any Yooper will tell you, road crews will have the main roads cleared and drivable within hours of even the biggest storm. Many roads in the U.P. see little traffic, and have limited cell phone coverage. Exercise caution and prepare accordingly!

FLYING
Two airports service this region; Sawyer International Airport (MQT) south of Marquette and Houghton County Memorial (CMX) in Hancock. Both are served by daily flights and offer a number of car rental options.

GEAR & RENTALS
Forget your boots back home? No worries! Down Wind Sports, with locations in Marquette and Houghton, is a full service climbing shop offering gear and clothing from the leading climbing manufacturers. They also have the largest selection of ice climbing rentals in the Midwest.

GUIDE SERVICE
For some folks, hiring a local guide for a day of climbing is an excellent way to experience some of the remote climbs in the U.P. If you are new to ice climbing, or would like to tick off a committing lakeshore climb like HMR, Michigan Ice Fest Guides is the premier ice climbing guide service in the U.P. Check them out at www.iceclimbmichigan.com

Houghton

Bergland

Bessemer Marquette Munising

Getting Around the UP the Easy Way
Mike Wilkinson

HISTORY

Isolated from the world by seas of fresh water, the Upper Peninsula has long been an area that attracts adventurous spirits. Hardy fur traders, miners, and lumbermen have all attempted to eke out a living in this sparsely populated region. Its wild and rugged nature has been romanticized by the likes of Ernest Hemingway and Jim Harrison.

Like the pioneers before them, hardy ice climbers have been exploring the backcountry of the U.P for decades, exploring the far reaches of the peninsula looking for the hidden treasure and deep solitude the region offers.

The ice in the U.P. remained relatively unknown outside of the small Midwestern ice climbing community. Starting in the late 1970's, this anonymity allowed early pioneers like Paul and Jude Kuenn, Dave Riggs, Mark Reisch, Tom Destri, Matt Manfredi, Andrew Tweddle, Val Buckley, Steve Darrell and Dennis Roscetti to foster an era of exploratory route development. With no published information, the only beta available was what they could gather through the grapevine of the other, highly-dispersed ice climbers around the Great Lakes. With so little to work with, they resorted to other sources. They found books on the waterfalls of Michigan, scoured the brochures for Pictured Rocks boat cruises and gathered beta from snowmobilers who had photos of amazing ice formations. They also poured over regional topo maps looking for possible routes to be climbed.

In December of 1979 the Kuenns were up on Munising Falls (before a boardwalk was built and subsequently demolished by a partial cliff collapse leading to the closure of climbing on the formation). By spring of 1980 they were outfitted for a week of snow and sub-zero temps and found at least 5 full rope length (150' in those days) leads along the shore between Sand Point and Grand Portal Point. The lake ice had excellent skiing and they had no idea there was a trail on top! It was on this trip that Paul did the FA of HMR. According to Paul:

> "The lake was frozen, skied out from the beach. One Wooden tool Piolet, one short tool. Bad Ass. Originally named "Singing in the Rain"... It was a late March ascent.... renamed HMR post 2012 or 13? Ice fest party weekend... Long story, find a man named Ross, he might just tell you all of it...or maybe not."

It was very typical of Paul and the early pioneers to climb climbs and not name or document them. Another one of those "finds" was a 50-meter grade 5 (Dairyland). With an approaching storm and all of their screws frozen up, temperatures dropping, and ice dinnerplating off, Paul made the first ascent of this ultra classic. Paul kids that it should have been called "Scared Shitless!" Paul's exploration continued into the late '80s and by the early '90s, Dairyland Expeditions, his climbing school based out of Appleton Wisconsin, was in full swing, bringing new climbers to the area.

Munising Snowshoe Club
1900
Unknown

In 1986, Mark Reisch and Dave Riggs made a pilgrimage to Ice Fest IV in Orient Bay in northern Ontario. Shaun Parent and crew were super welcoming to the two Americans and the camaraderie of the festival and the community of climbers inspired Mark to try to replicate the Orient Bay scene in Munising. To that end, in November 1990, Mark wrote up and mailed out to all the contacts in his little notebook the first issue of the *Great Lakes Ice Climbing Newsletter* which read, "The goal of this newsletter is to provide the ice climbers from around the Great Lakes region with a way to communicate with each other and share information." A photocopied, two sided sheet of paper, with basic info on known and possible ice venues around the Great Lakes and some other info. That was it. In the "Events & Trips" section was a listing for "Michigan Ice Fest, Date ?" That date ended up being January 19 and 20, 1991. In the third issue of the *Great Lakes Ice Climbing Newsletter* (November 1991), Mark reported that 26 people attended the first Michigan Ice Fest. He must have counted every local and visiting snowmobiler in the bar at Ziegert's because there were maybe ten ice climbers there, but like the Orient Bay Ice Fest, it was super fun. Mark gave each attendee at that first Michigan Ice Festival a copy of his *Guidebook to Ice Climbing in the Upper Peninsula of Michigan,* with its one page of formations and areas around Munising and on Grand Island and its marked photocopy of a map from the National Lakeshore brochure.

Munising Falls (now closed)
Paul Kuenn
Paul Kuen Collection

Grand Island circa 1980
Paul & Jude Kuenn, and Scott Hauser
Paul Kuenn Collection

Paul's exploration and Mark's organizing efforts laid the foundation for the next generation of climbers. Enter Bill and Arni.

In winter of 1991 Arni Ronis and Bill Thompson were beginning to explore the ice formations in Marquette, Eben and, on a whim, decided to attend the Michigan Ice Festival. They walked into Sydney's to find a small gathering watching a Shaun Parent sideshow on the restaurant wall, complete with waitresses walking through the presentation! After a weekend of climbing, they were welcomed into this small fold of climbers and it was the true beginning of their love of ice climbing and the festival. By 1995, the two took over from Mark and began organizing the festival, intertwining their love of ice climbing and the joy of sharing those experiences. In 1998, Thompson produced a small guidebook, *Michigan Ice! An Ice Climbers Guide to the Central Upper Peninsula of Michigan*, which documented 57 of the more common routes in and around Pictured Rocks.

Even in the post "olden age" there was a keen sense of discovery and exploration. Without the Internet and blogging, every day out had the excitement of being a "first". If Bill hadn't climbed it, or known who did, it hadn't been done! The community was small and if you saw a car with climbing stickers in the parking lot at Sand Point, you followed their tracks. Ice climbing was a true dark art and in the late 1990s Andy Albosta, James Loveridge and Corey Papenhagen wanted the secrets. With athletic ability and strong minds the trio ticked off the classics and put up many bold ascents including the committing Strawberry Daze and Split Lip. Keeping true to area tradition, many of their ascents went unrecorded

Sometime in the early 2000s Jon Jugenheimer and Joe Mucci began their long weekend commutes from southern Wisconsin to the Upper Peninsula, with their forte being exploring the deepest regions of PRNL. The long drives, followed by a long ski, and camping along the shoreline paid off for the two as they picked off lines from Chapel Beach east to Spray Falls. With a wealth of new climbs Jon published *An Ice Climbers Guide to Munising Michigan* in 2007. Combining their passion for the area and love of its history, Jon and Bill combined forces to produce a 3rd edition of the guidebook in 2012 that included many new routes, maps and local information.

25 years later he still has the same helmet
Arni Ronis ✗
Bill Thompson 📷

Starting in 2013, local film maker Aaron Peterson of Clear & Cold Cinema, began working on the documentary The Michigan Ice Film, telling the untold story of the long ignored climbing mecca and the strange scrappy people who are drawn to it. The release was a huge success and kick-started the outside world's discovery of ice climbing in the Munising area. During this same time period Hollywood found their way to Pictured Rocks. In honor of their centennial, the National Park Service was making an IMAX film following legendary mountaineer Conrad Anker on his adventures through the parks. Originally the crew was slated to shoot the winter scenes in Yellowstone, but due to a paltry snowfall and warmer-than-usual temperatures the shoot was canceled. At the same time, the release of the Michigan Ice Film was hitting the Internet and the scenes caught the attention of the directors and the winter location was quickly changed. According to producer Shaun MacGillivray:

> "We'd never seen a place that looked so much like a fantasy land— where you have caves filled with ice crystals and icy waterfalls that are so pristine. It's a real hidden gem and it was a chance for us to explore the wild in winter. It was even a new experience for Conrad, Rachel and Max and we found the place had a tremendous emotional resonance."

With the release of these films, and a third film by Red Bull Media a few years later, a floodgate of publicity was opened illustrating the amazing climbing potential the area offers and it helped to solidify Pictured Rocks National Lakeshore as a premier ice climbing destination in the country. Today an influx of talented climbers are traveling to the U.P. to explore the remote difficult lines and hone their skills on the area test pieces. It's ushered in a new age of exploration. Climbers are trekking deeper into the wild places and finding for themselves the amazing ice hidden around the next bend. They may not be finding first ascents, but in a nod to the early pioneers of the area they are certainly finding first experiences.

Racking up in the '80s
Paul Kuenn
Paul Kuen Collection

Organizer of the first Ice Fest
Mark Reisch
Paul Kuenn Collection

GEOLOGY

The geology of the Upper Peninsula of Michigan is complex and spans eons of time and hundreds of miles east to west. In the western U.P. and Keweenaw Peninsula, complex igneous rocks over a billion years old were formed as a direct result of the mid-continent rift which is partly responsible for forming Lake Superior. Subsequent erosion and deposition of sediments formed by those rocks also have interest to climbers and are primarily found along Lake Superior's south shore. In the central and far eastern U.P. a much younger (400-500 million years old) sedimentary rock composed primarily of limestone rims the large basin of Lower Michigan.

Climbers looking for ice don't just care about the rock, but hydrology as well. How water moves through, or over the rock and then freezes on the surface is what interests us, and that interaction between rock, water and freezing temperatures is what makes this place so magical.

Pictured Rocks National Lakeshore is composed of two Cambrian aged sandstone units called the Munising and the Au Train formations. These units were formed about 50 million years apart, and form the cliffs found from Grand Island to the eastern reaches of the park. Tannin stained ground water is constantly moving through the rock, pulling dissolved minerals and precipitating them on the cliff walls to make the beautiful green, black, red and pink colors that make up what the area is known for. The ice climbing found in Pictured Rocks is formed by both ground water freezing into the "seep" style routes and surface water pouring off the top creating waterfall routes. *The Curtains* are formed by ground water flowing out of the rock, whereas *The Dryerhose* is formed by surface water pouring over the top.

The igneous rocks in the western U.P. are both intrusive and extrusive volcanic rocks, primarily basalt and rhyolite. The main difference between much of the ice in the western U.P. and the ice found in PRNL is that it is created from surface water, not groundwater. Snow melt and surface water cascade and drip over the tops of the hardened, fractured cliffs and form white and blue ice, rather than the yellow tannin rich ice of Munising.

The Amphitheater
X Unknown
📷 Michael Tokarz

ECOLOGY

The Upper Peninsula is predominantly covered by northern hardwood forests. made up of maple, birch, beech (only in the eastern half), white pine and hemlock trees. In the late 1800s and early 1900s the forests were logged for timber leaving few old trees and covering the landscape with a second growth forest characterized by smaller trees and a trend toward fast growing species. Timber is still an major part of the local economy and acts as an important management tool for our forests.

Wetlands are also prevalent throughout the peninsula creating a diverse habitat with ash, spruce, cedar and tamarack trees, as well as a variety of undergrowth you probably won't see while out climbing due to the snow. These wetlands provide the water for many of our favorite climbs. The decaying leaves and organic matter of these thick forests leave tannins which stain the water a rich reddish brown, providing the distinctive color seen so frequently in the climbs of the U.P.

The large tracts of undeveloped forest have created a haven for wildlife with nearly 300 species of vertebrates including 42 mammals and 182 birds. You're most likely to spot deer, squirrels and a myriad of birds but if you luck out you might see moose or even a black bear waking up after a long winter.

Winter is a slow time for most plants and animals in the north since short days and cold temperatures reduce the activity of pretty much everyone except ice climbers.

Just like everywhere else on the planet, the Upper Peninsula is not immune to the impacts of humans. The arrival of invasive species has had a huge impact on the vegetation (beech bark disease, emerald ash borer, garlic mustard, etc.). The rising water temperature of Lake Superior and the increasing frequency of extreme weather events caused by climate change, as well as constant land use pressure will have profound, long term impacts on the region. Doing our best to be good stewards in every aspect of our lives will help this region as well as our entire planet.

Alces alces
Bill Thompson

RULES, REGULATIONS AND ETHICS

Climbing areas are not just unique because of their rock or ice, but the culture that surrounds them. The rules and ethics of the area set the tone and underlie all parts of the experience when climbing.

The U.P. is one of the friendliest places you'll ever visit. The locals will do whatever they can to make your visit as special as the place you're visiting. That's the ethic here. Be kind. Remember that everyone else's experience is just as important as your own. Share your climbs, share your knowledge and share the good times. A nice word and a friendly gesture go a long way. Seeing other climbers smiling is a great indicator that you're doing it right.

This ethic of kindness extends beyond your fellow climbers and the people that call this area home. The landscape and environment in the U.P. are as much a part of the character as the people and the ice. It's all of our responsibilities to make sure this character is unblemished. Pick up after yourself, and when you're done with that, pick up after someone else. Minimize your impact on the environment and leave everywhere you go better than you found it.

Be mindful that your use of the land is impacting someone else's experience. You're not the only one out there. Dogs, loud music, and excessive celebration affect the other users in the area. Please use discretion. This is a quiet, calm place.

Many of the climbs in the Upper Peninsula have access issues or rely on private land for access. Please, respect landowners. Trespassing, in addition to being a crime, is a great way to ensure we'll never gain access. We've done our best to include any issues in this guide but circumstances do change so please heed any posted warnings or call Down Wind Sports in Marquette for the latest information.

Public land is a major component of the wild and remote feel of the U.P. These lands are managed by many different agencies. The National Park Service, Forest Service, Department of Natural Resources, and others all have differing rules and regulations. It is up to you to know where you are, know the rules, and follow them. The penalties for not following the rules vary but one thing is for sure: we all represent our entire community and the fastest way to ruin our relationship with these management agencies is through poor behavior. Your actions impact every other climber so do everything you can to have a positive impact.

Oh, and have fun. That's a rule, too.

West Shore of Trout Bay
Emily Oppliger
Erik Olsen

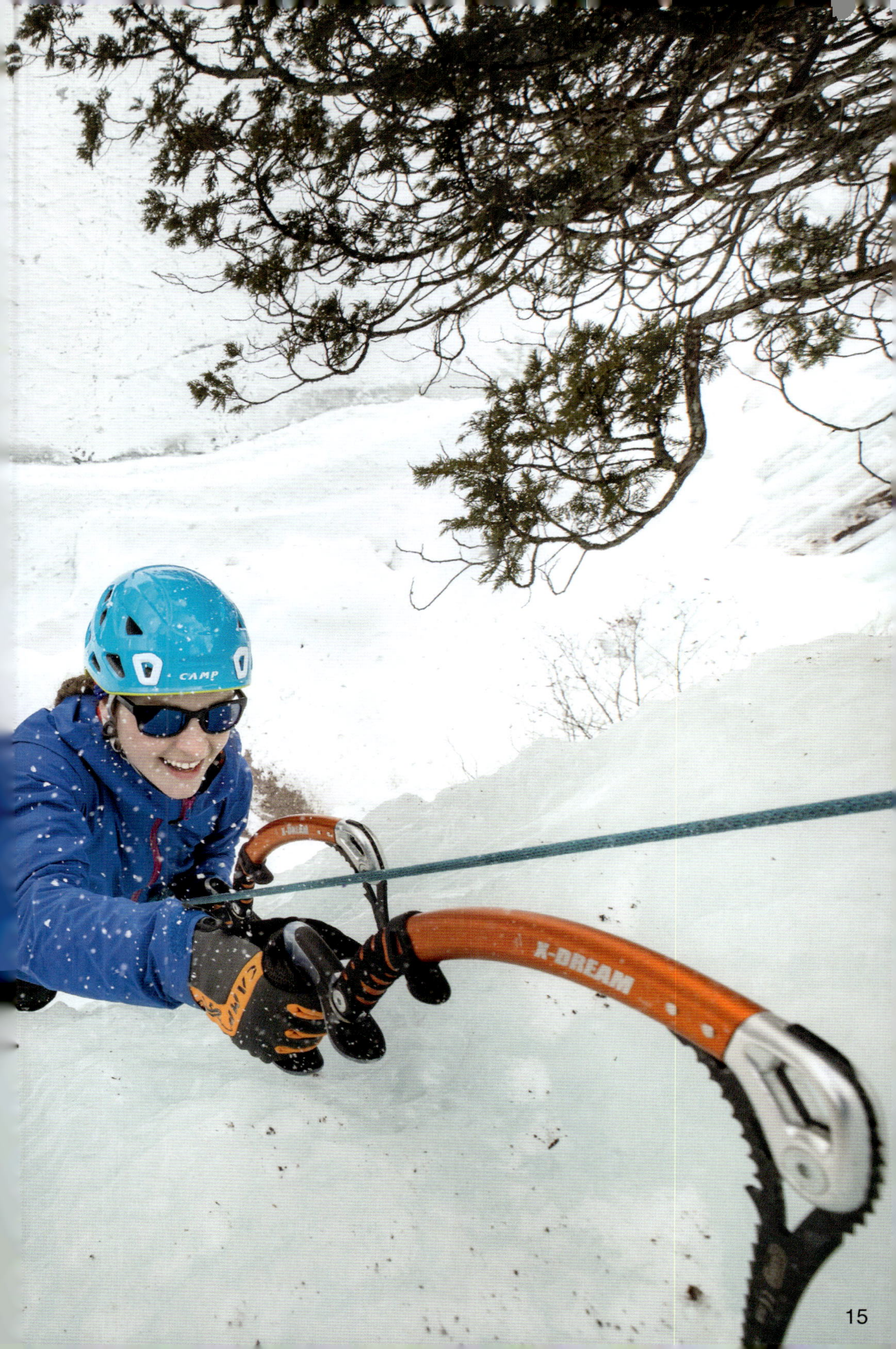
CAMP
X-DREAM

MICHIGAN ICE FEST

Quietly nestled on the south shore of Lake Superior sits one of the country's largest concentrations of ice. For years it was an undiscovered secret treasure that very few climbers had ever heard of. Then the secret got out. Climbers began to discover what many of us have known for decades: Michigan ice climbing is phenomenal and The Michigan Ice Fest is at the epicenter of it all!

The festival, the longest running ice climbing festival in the country, was started by a handful of hearty souls who had a distinct love for the area and were interested in sharing their passion with others. Tales of the pillars of ice spread and a tribe of climbers bonded over cold ice, even colder beer and we became something of a family. Over the years our family of climbers has grown a lot. We are no longer seven people watching a slide-show in a bar, we're now over 1,000 close- knit climbers watching presentations from some of the world's most talented athletes in a beautiful historic theater!

Bill Thompson preaching the gospel on stage at the fest
Mike Wilkinson

Illicit fireworks display!
Mike Wilkinson

Whether you're an experienced climber who's been to every Michigan Ice Fest, or an adventure seeker who's never tied into a rope, there's something for you at the event. The festival makes ice climbing accessible to the first timer, teaches advanced skills to those looking to improve and connects participants with the greater climbing community.

This is a special place where you can socialize and bond as climbers and get together as the biggest, most fun family anywhere. We invite you to come on up to the Upper Peninsula to experience this extraordinary event where you can expect to experience our famed "Yooper" hospitality and world-class ice.

FOR MORE INFORMATION CHECK OUT
MICHIGANICEFEST.COM

Celebrating another Ice Fest
Mike Wilkinson

Thinking About Ice
Adam Dailey & Jon Jugenheimer
Mike Wilkinson

ICE BETA:
HOW TO USE THIS GUIDE

This guidebook is broken into two parts: the first and primary focus of this guide is Pictured Rocks National Lakeshore and second is the rest of the Upper Peninsula. Pictured Rocks is the epicenter of ice climbing in Middle America. The rest of the Upper Peninsula is more of a hidden gem and deserves to be climbed more frequently. Take a moment to study all of what this guide has to offer and seek out new adventures along the entire Lake Superior snowbelt.

This climbing guide is laid out geographically, where the climbs are listed right to left, or north to south depending on the specific area and approach direction to the climbs. We have gone to every length possible to provide you with the best known way to approach and provide GPS locations to all the climbs listed in this book. That being said, there may be an error, or three, so please accept our apologies and chalk it up to a new adventure, not a failed attempt on one specific route.

The most philosophical beta we can give is to highlight that there are no First Ascent names listed in this guidebook. We have neglected the traditional use of listing the FA for each climb based on the complex (often times confusing) climbing history of the area, the multifaceted nature of the climbing found along the lakeshore and a personal ethic of one man in particular, Paul Kuenn (PK). PK has probably authored more FAs in the U.P. than anyone will ever know, but he never cared to record them, which is his personal choice and an ethos that has slowly crept into the subconscious of the ice climbers in this region.

PK believes in "First Experiences" not FAs, and that everyone can have a FE any time they head out to a new area, whereas a FA can only happen once. In some popular climbing destinations, once a climb forms for the season it becomes a frozen pegboard, picked out from multiple ascents, and the grade usually drops at least a whole number. Once you get past the climbs located along Sand Point Road, you will always find virgin ice, never picked out and always in the same condition as the FA. The challenges that were found on the backcountry pillars of yesteryear, are the same challenges you can test yourself against today.

Currently there are more climbs than climbers in the UP, and you can always find a First Experience every time you go out to the likes of Grand Island, Norwich Ledge, or to the classic *Dairyland* (yeah, PK climbed that first, and it took Bill Thompson to name the route in his honor!), all you have to do is walk further than 30 minutes from the car and the day will be yours forever.

GRADING ICE

Grading climbs, and ice climbs especially, is a subjective matter than can be debated endlessly. Ice is a plastic medium, it can change every season or even every day. The ice a leader sees is not the same ice the person following sees. It can become chopped up and kicked out by even one climber.

That being said, grading climbs is important. It gives a reference point for our progress as climbers and helps keep us from getting in over our heads.

This guide does its best to grade the climbs accurately, but remember to take these grades for what they are, just a reference point. Use your own judgment and enjoy your first experience.

Water Ice grades are broken down into a scale from 1 to 6, with the letters WI proceeding the number standing for Water Ice. As each route in this book is graded between WI1 to WI6, that grade denotes the climb in average condition, on an average year and does not take ice protection into the equation in this guide. You may find a route in this guide harder, or easier than the grade given on any particular day, which is typical for this ever-changing, ethereal, evaporative, ephemeral medium we climb.

WI1: *Low angle, ice tools are usually not required.*

WI2: *60° ice with possible bulges.*

WI3: *Consistent 70° ice, or short climbs (<10 M) with vertical ice of 80-90°.*

WI4: *Continuous 80° ice, with steps of vertical ice on longer climbs. Good rest stances can be found.*

WI5: *Entire pitch of near 90° ice or vertical ice with few good rests, the climb is long and strenuous.*

WI6: *90° technical ice, possible wild, wind blown features, or thin pillars. Arduous climbing the entire pitch.*

Lakeshore Curtains WI2

The Curtains WI3

The Dryer Hose WI4

HMR WI5

USING THE MAPS

Front Country
Lakeshore Trail
Miners to Mosquito
Mosquito to Chapel
Chapel East
Inland
East Channel
Trout Bay
West Shore
North Shore
Rock River Canyon
Marquette Co.
Copper Country
Western U.P.

MAP SYMBOLS
- NPS headquarters
- Trailhead
- Parking
- Campground
- Bathroom
- Hospital
- Lighthouse
- Ferry Dock

Finding and identifying climbs can be tough. There is A LOT of ice out there and knowing what's what is important. We've included maps and GPS coordinates to help you in this task but please note that we cannot guarantee 100% accuracy of these. They are for reference only and should not be relied on as your sole means of navigation.

All GPS coordinates are presented in decimal degrees in the WGS84 coordinate system. The scale varies from map to map, but is indicated on each map in both metric and imperial units.

The maps and climbs are color-coded by region to help you find the area you're interested in more easily.

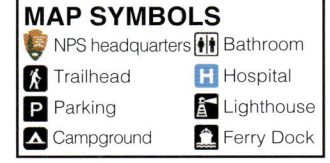

DISCLAIMER

Climbing is a dangerous activity. This book is in no way a substitute for instruction or experience. The reader of this guide assumes full responsibility for his or her climbing actions. The authors, publishers and distributors are not responsible for any event resulting in injury or death. You should not depend on any information obtained from this book for your personal safety; ultimately your safety depends on your experience, good judgment and your climbing abilities. If there are any doubts as to the abilities of your party to safely set up a climb or to attempt a route in this book, do not attempt it.

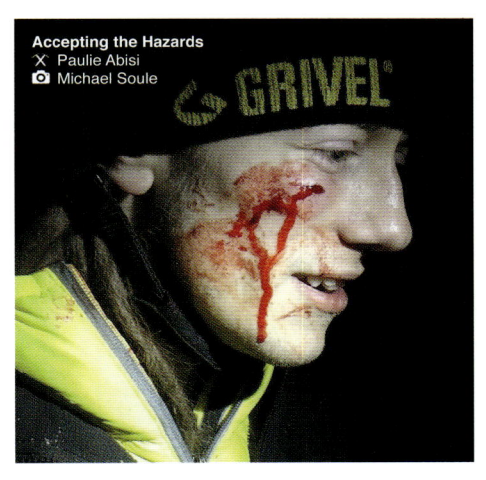

Accepting the Hazards
X Paulie Abisi
◉ Michael Soule

The use of this book indicates your acceptance of the risks associated with the activity of ice climbing and the acknowledgment of responsibility for your own safety and well being.

You, and only you, are responsible for yourself, climb safe!

PICTURED ROCKS &

With one of the largest concentrations of climbable ice in the country, and a huge lake that sets it apart from any other climbing area, Pictured Rocks and Grand Island are the premier destination for ice climbers in the Midwest.

Hundreds of climbs ranging from WI2 to WI6+ provide almost endless options for the adventurous climber. Access to climbs can be as simple as walking 100 yards off the road, or as adventurous as riding a snowmobile across the lake or skiing all day through silent forests. The area holds the vast majority of ice climbs in the Upper Peninsula and if you can only visit one spot, this is the one.

GRAND ISLAND

HMR
Conrad Anker
Mike Wilkinson

Stretching 50 miles northeast of Munising, Pictured Rocks National Lakeshore hosts many of the classic climbs and is the most accessible. Sitting just offshore in Munising Bay, Grand Island is often out of reach due to lake ice conditions. But when the lake freezes and it's safe to cross, it's the place to be, offering the best climbing and a sense of wild remoteness that's hard to find in the world today.

The town of Munising sits as the hub for this spectacular place and an ice climber could hardly want a better basecamp. It offers a great small town feel with friendly locals, fun bars and enough snow and cold to satisfy any winter lover.

THINGS TO KNOW

Lakeshore Safety

Climbing over a fresh water sea adds an extra element of both excitement and risk. When climbing along the lakeshore please make sure your group has the skills required for self-rescue. Once you rap over the edge you have to be able to climb out or to ascend the rope. One thing to consider before gearing up for a longer lakeshore route is whether to climb with leashes or an umbilical. If you're leading one of these lakeshore routes, dropping a tool would be disastrous. Consider "leashing up" if you are leading out over the lake.

Situated just offshore of the mainland, Grand Island offers 28 miles of shoreline, much of it 60m cliffs, with stunning routes. Inaccessible unless the lake freezes and ice is sufficiently formed. Skiing, snowshoeing or snowmobiling are the preferred methods of accessing the island but can be very dangerous! While it might be tempting to make the short crossing from Sand Point to the East Channel, it is NEVER advisable as strong currents in the channel affect the lake ice thickness. Cross instead from the Grand Island public access and follow the Grand Island shoreline to the East Channel. Please check with the Park Service or local climbers before venturing out on the lake ice!

Approaches

Snowshoes or no snowshoes? The big question is whether to bring them or not. If you are planning to climb along the lakeshore, throw them in the car just in case. By mid-season there is a packed trail leading out to the climbs located along the shore, but it is not uncommon for Lake Superior snow storms to bury that path in 30 plus inches! Headed to Grand Island? For purists it's a no-brainer. Pack the skis, put your head down and rack up the kilometers. The only problem is that if you're not winter camping and you want to hit the north shore, it's damn near impossible to do so. But a snowmobile or four wheeler can get you ice climbing before the Nordic skier gets to the island!

Don't have a machine? No problem. There are several rental facilities in Munising that will rent by the day or weekend. Pick up your rig, head out Miners Castle Road and your party will be amazed at the endless amounts of ice to climb. As always, check with locals before venturing onto the lake ice.

Winter Camping

While most climbers will opt for a warm bed and a cold beer after climbing, the hardy will turn towards the tent and a sunrise rising out of Lake Superior to start their day. Be warned, the Upper Peninsula of Michigan is a winter paradise, which means lots of snow and the possibility of brutal temperatures. BE PREPARED!

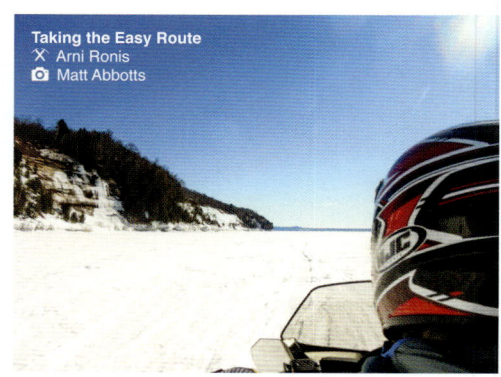

Taking the Easy Route
X Arni Ronis
📷 Matt Abbotts

Pictured Rocks National Lakeshore Regulations

- A backcountry camping permit is required year-round at Pictured Rocks National Lakeshore. The fee is $5 per person, per night ($15 reservation fee). Permits must be obtained via www.recreation.gov or by calling 1-877-444-6777.
- A snow depth of 6 inches or more is required for winter camping rules to take effect.
- Winter camping is permitted in drive-in campgrounds without charge.
- Winter camping is permitted off park roads beyond a distance of 100 feet.
- Use of stoves is required. Campfires are not permitted unless you build them in fire rings in developed front or backcountry sites.
- Winter camping is permitted beyond 100 feet of a creek, river or lake.
- Overnight camping in parking lots is not permitted.
- Drytooling and mixed climbing are not allowed in the park, or Grand Island.

Important Contact Information

PICTURED ROCKS NATIONAL LAKESHORE
1505 Sand Point Rd.
Munising, MI 49862
906-387-3700

MUNISING MEMORIAL HOSPITAL
1500 Sand Point Rd.
Munising, MI 49862
906-387-4110

ALGER COUNTY SHERIFF
101 Court St.
Munising, MI 49862
906-387-4444

DENTAL ASSOCIATES
Emergency Dental Work
416 Mill St
Munising, MI 49862
906-387-3704

DOWN WIND SPORTS
Ice Conditions/Climbing Gear
514 N. Third St.
Marquette, MI 49855
906-226-7112
downwindsports.com

WILDERNESS RECOVERY
Towing
109 E Munising Ave,
Munising, MI 49862
(906) 202-1336

FRONT COUNTRY

The Curtains
X James Loveridge
📷 Bill Thompson

FRONT COUNTRY   21 ROUTES • WI2–5 • 6–23m

The front country is the closest ice to Munising. With short approaches and a plethora of climbs in the WI2 to WI4 range, it is one of the best places to learn how to swing an ice tool in the Midwest. *The Dryer Hose*, *The Amphitheater*, *The Curtains*, and *Twin Falls* are all classics and should be on everyone's tick list.

The front country is accessed off Sand Point Road east of downtown. There is no parking along Sand Point Road so drive to the end, park in the lot, and walk the road back to your climb.

Map

GRAND ISLAND

LAKE SUPERIOR

EAST CHANNEL LIGHTHOUSE

EAST CHANNEL

PARK HEADQUARTERS

THREE SISTERS
INTERSECTION FALLS

BIG PINE PILLAR
SWAMP THING
STEEP SEEP OF 3
SAND POINT FALLS
SWAMP CURTAINS

THE SCHOOLROOM
TEACHER SAYS
NO BOUNDARIES
DRAKE SEEP

THE AMPHITHEATER

THE DRYER HOSE

THE CURTAINS
BOOMER FALLS
OPENING CURTAIN
CURTAIN CALL
PRELUDE CURTAIN
FINAL ACT

MUNISING BAY

TWIN FALLS

LITTLE ONE

WINDOW WALTZ
MEMORIAL FALLS

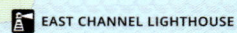

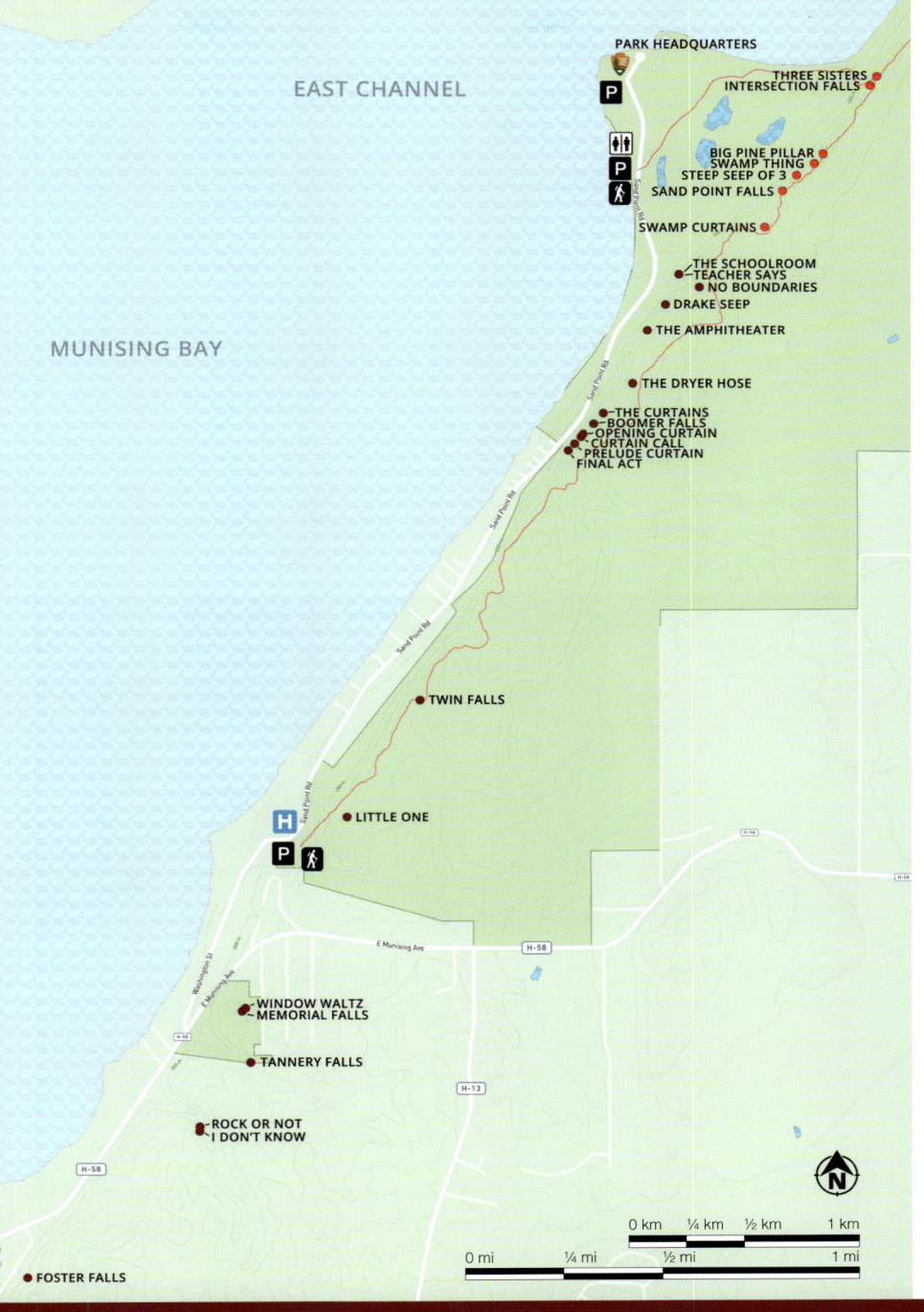

TANNERY FALLS

ROCK OR NOT
I DON'T KNOW

FOSTER FALLS

0 km ¼ km ½ km 1 km
0 mi ¼ mi ½ mi 1 mi

FRONT COUNTRY

Foster Falls ☐
WI3   7 meters   N46.4076 W86.6384

From Munising travel on highway H58 east past the paper plant and across the Anna River. Turn right on Foster Street and park at the dead end. Climb half way up the power line and head north along the ridge.

A fun, short climb that resembles many of the front country climbs that form in a sandstone bowl. Please be respectful as this climb is situated in a neighborhood.

Window Waltz ☐
WI3   7 meters   N46.4176 W86.6270

This short climb forms around the corner to the north of Memorial Falls.

Be sure to check out the climb through a "window" in the sandstone between the two climbs.

Memorial Falls ☐
WI3   10 meters   N46.4175 W86.6271

This climb has the easiest access and shortest approach of any climb in Munising. Drive east from town on H58 and continue past Washington Street (Sand Point Road). Turn right on Nestor Street and travel two blocks south. Park on the right side of the street at a sign for the *Memorial Falls* trail head. The trail is 0.4 miles long, and brings you to the top of the falls. Follow the trail around and down to the bottom for easy access.

Tannery Falls ☐
WI3   12 meters   N446.4156 W86.6267

Tannery Creek fans out over the sandstone and proceeds to fall 12 meters to the floor below. A sheet of ice forms consistently early in the season every year.

Window Waltz
Jon Jugenheimer X
Aaron Peterson 📷

Rock Or Not ☐
WI3   10 meters   N46.4132 W86.6293

A short climb that forms into a sheet of ice with a few variations possible depending on the season.

I Don't Know ☐
WI3   6 meters   N46.4131 W86.6294

Several ice fangs that form to climber's left of *Rock or Not*. They can make for interesting but short climbing.

Editors Note: *Memorial Falls*, *Tannery Falls* and *Window Waltz* are closed for climbing at the time of printing. Please respect this. For updated information please call Down Wind Sports.

Munsing Falls

Munsing Falls is permanently closed to climbing via Pictured Rocks National Lakeshore's policy. This is the only closed climb in the park, respect it.

Little One ☐
WI3　　　　　　　　　6 meters　　　　　　　　N46.4247 W86.6216

Little One is the first climb along Sand Point Road coming from town. Park at the *Munsing Falls* parking area and walk the road north until you see a packed trail across the street from Harborview Assisted Living. Turn east into the woods on this packed trail and gradually climb up to a trail intersection. Turn south (right) and walk the trail a short distance where you will see the sandstone bowl and *Little One*.

Twin Falls
Unknown ✗
Mike Wilkinson 📷

Twin Falls ☐
WI3　　　　　　　　　10 meters　　　　　　　　N46.4290 W86.6178

Continuing up the packed trail past *Little One*, the trail tops out in an old apple orchard. Follow the Lakeshore Trail to access the PRNL ski trail. Please walk to the side of the groomed trail. Climbers will approach the climbs from the top where *Left Twin* will first come into view.

The two spectacular pillars are located in a large sandstone cave. *Right Twin* is the steeper but shorter of the two climbs, while *Left Twin* is a more technical, two tiered pillar.

FRONT COUNTRY

Curtains Area
X Amber Munoz
📷 Michael Tokarz

Prelude Curtain ☐
WI3   7 meters
N46.4385 W86.6098

The furthest curtain from the Sand Point parking lot, this climb is tucked into the woods near the snowplow turnaround. Ascend this small chunk of ice to an alcove in the cedar trees.

Opening Curtain ☐
WI3   9 meters
N46.4388 W86.6093

Easily spotted from the road, this wide sheet of ice is formed by water that constantly drips through a wide muddy gully.

Final Act ☐
WI2   6 meters
N46.4383 W86.6101

A small flow located at a slight depression in the cliffline, the *Final Act* is hopefully not yours, but rather a great climb for the novice climber.

Curtain Call ☐
WI3   7 meters
N46.4388 W86.6094

Nearly a replica of *The Curtains*, but narrower, this flow is a classic and can usually hold more than one rope all season.

Boomer Falls ☐
WI3   8 meters   N46.4392 W86.6087

The old story being passed around about this climb is that its name is a verb, not a noun and yes, Boomer is OK, less his ego. One of the longer climbs located west of *The Curtains*, it's a great target to hit when traversing the cliffline ticking off routes.

The Curtains ☐
WI3   6–10 meters   N46.4396 W86.6082

This beautiful curtain of blue ice extends 100 feet and can be seen from the road. It is one of the most popular climbing areas in Munising due to its quick access, variety of climbs and easy top access.

Class at the Curtains during the 2018 Michigan Ice Fest
📷 Jacob Raab

The Dryer Hose
Jon Jugenheimer ✗
Matt Abbotts 📷

The Dryer Hose
WI4　　　　　23 meters　　　　　N46.4409 W86.6070

Climbing up the approach trail and catching the first glimpse of *The Dryer Hose* can be awe-inspiring. *The Dryer Hose* is a classic route in Munising, a must do pillar on everyone's tick list. This climb is a large freestanding pillar that forms in a typical Pictured Rocks sandstone bowl. The base is usually cauliflowered, leading to a vertical pillar and a flat top out. Large trees above the climb can be used to make multiple anchors.

FRONT COUNTRY

Ode to The Dryer Hose

Way up in the old U.P.
Just out of Mew-ni-sing
There rose a pitch of water ice
A beauty to be seen.

It hung from a lip with air all 'round.
Stood tall as a lean white birch.
To gaze at it and contemplate
Was like a prayer in church.

Tall and fine, its cold crystals set
Straight as a drop of water falls.
To take the sharp end up that path
Really took some … er … nerve!

Alas, and now it wears a "skirt";
Its steepness lost to fools.
Today some dance upon its flanks
Without even using tools!

Old memories long for the day,
When challenge it would pose.
But now it's just an "easy day",
Since someone took The Hose.

Yes, Way up in the old U.P.
At Ice Fest it still flows.
But, the thrill will never be the same,
Since someone took The Hose.

Phil Watts

The Dryer Hose
Angela Vanwiemeersch
Jon Jugenheimer

Originally named *Life's A Pitch*, the climb took its new name from a well-placed clothes dryer hose that was used by some creative climbers to redirect the water from a small stream over an undercut sandstone edge to form a better climb. When the Pictured Rocks National Park administration decided to actively promote ice climbing, they removed the dryer hose and the climb was renamed to celebrate its proud place in the history of early ice farming.

The Amphitheater
Katie McKinstry X
Joe Stylos 📷

The Amphitheater ☐
WI5 20 meters N46.4419 W86.6069

This climb usually forms a small pencil-like pillar that rises to meet a series of cascading hanging daggers hanging across the lip of the roof above. When the climb does touch down, delicate climbing is necessary to ascend the dead vertical pillar.

Drake Seep ☐
WI3 6 meters
N46.4437 W86.6049

Short and steep, this small section of ice is accessed 50 feet southwest of the *No Boundaries* trailhead. Walk straight back through the woods to the sandstone wall and this blue ice.

No Boundaries ☐
WI3 10 meters
N46.4444 W86.6032

One of the closest climbs to the Sand Point Road parking lot, this sheet of ice sees little action throughout the year. A short snowshoe into this box canyon brings one into view of this peaceful ice formation.

The Amphitheater
X Bill Thompson
📷 Linda Wappner

FRONT COUNTRY

Schoolroom
Colten Moore
Bill Thompson

Schoolroom
WI3   8 meters   N46.4449 W86.6042

Schoolroom is a secluded climbing area offering a variety of climbing lines; perfect for small groups and beginner climbers. Access this area via the *No Boundaries* trailhead where you will travel northeast along the sandstone cliff until the ice comes into view.

Teacher Says
WI2   6 meters   N46.4449 W86.6042

More of an access gully on the far right of *Schoolroom* than an actual climb, this low-angle ice offers beginners the chance to get on something less than vertical — a rarity in Munising!

Swamp Thing
David Hixenbaugh
Bill Thompson

LAKESHORE TRAIL

Looking across the historic lighthouse on Grand Island
📷 Mike Wilkinson

LAKESHORE TRAIL   43 ROUTES • WI2–6 • 3–60m

The Lakeshore Trail is the second-most popular region of Pictured Rocks for climbers and it offers the quickest access to climbs over Lake Superior. Park at the Sand Point parking lot, then follow the trail exiting the east side of the parking area until it climbs a large staircase and joins the North Country Trail. The vast majority of the climbs are found by taking a left at the intersection found at the top of the staircase. There is usually a packed trail all the way from the parking lot to at least *Dairyland*, so flotation is usually not needed. Finding many of these climbs from the top can be tricky.

LAKE SUPERIOR

- MIDNIGHT RAMBLER
- LEFT SODA STRAW
- THE GOOD, THE BAD & THE UGLY
- THE CURTAIN CLIM
- SUCK IT UP
- TURTLE POWER
- SUNNY DAY
- MINI ME
- A MAN AND A HORSE
- GIDDY UP
- HI HO SILVER
- KEMOSABE
- SWEET MOTHER MOSES

EAST CHANNEL

- ICE 10
- ICE 9
- CALUMET GIRLS
- THE ART OF SEDUCTION
- APRIL ICE IS NICE
- SHEET OF ICE
- TOTALLY TODD
- LAKESHORE CURTAINS
- THREE SISTERS
- INTERSECTION FALLS

PARK HEADQUARTERS

- BIG PINE PILLAR
- SWAMP THING
- STEEP SEEP OF 3
- SAND POINT FALLS
- SWAMP CURTAINS

To access the first 10 climbs along the Lakeshore Trail, instead of hiking to the top of the cliff at the big hill, turn northeast below the cliff band and traverse to find the routes. They are all hard to find from above, whereas walking along the base will let you take your pick of the lines in best condition. There are plenty of places to scramble to the top to set up a toprope once you have found what you are looking for. To access the routes *Sweet Mother Moses* and beyond, it is best to ascend to the top of the stairs and follow the Lakeshore Trail above the cliff the entire way.

LAKESHORE TRAIL

Steep Seep of 3 — Colten Moore — Bill Thompson

Swamp Curtain ☐
WI3   7 meters
N46.4469 W86.5996

The third bowl in a series located along the Lakeshore Trail southwest of *Intersection Falls*, it gives climbers another option to hone their skills on a short curtain.

Sand Point Falls ☐
WI3   7 meters
N46.4480 W86.5989

An obvious, deep drainage located along the Lakeshore Trail leads to this steep narrow pillar. Rap from the top to access this short climb.

Steep Seep of 3 ☐
WI3   7 meters
N46.4486 W86.5981

Three distinct thin seeps form side-by-side on this sheer vertical wall. Delicate start moves are required to gain the curtain above.

Best accessed from below via the *No Boundaries* trailhead.

Swamp Thing ☐
WI4   10 meters   N46.4489 W86.5969

Easily found by the enormous pine tree just off the Lakeshore Trail, this climb forms an overhanging curtain narrowing to a small pillar near the ground. Cauliflower to chandelier type ice makes Swamp Thing a bold lead.

Big Pine Pillar ☐
WI3   7 meters   N46.4493 W86.5968

Marked by three large pine trees at the top, this curtain is steep and fat! For those leading, access from the bottom is quite easy as you will follow the sandstone cliff to the right before *Intersection Falls*.

Intersection Falls ☐
WI2   4 meters
N46.4514 W86.5941

More of a landmark than a climb. A small piece of ice at the side of the stairs at the intersection of the trails.

Three Sisters ☐
WI3   7 meters
N46.4522 W86.5940

A sheet of ice around the corner (NE) from the last staircase to the Lakeshore Trail. It forms as three pillars that connect into a curtain at the top.

Three Sisters — Bill Thompson — Bill Thompson

Lakeshore Curtains ☐
WI3 6 meters
N46.4533 W86.5931

These curtains drop off the bluff intermittently for a quarter of a mile towards the northeast.

Totally Todd ☐
WI3 8 meters
N46.4542 W86.5923

Gruff and ornery, climb this short sheet of ice to the belay tree at the top.

Sheet of Ice ☐
WI3 7 meters
N46.4539 W86.5926

This creatively named climb is a sheet of ice about 13m wide.

April Ice is Nice ☐
WI3 9 meters N46.4544 W86.5920

Tucked back in the shadows of the bluff, this ice remains climbable well into April. Vertical for the first 7 meters and the last 2 meters are a mellow ramp.

The Art of Seduction
Linda Wappner
Bill Thompson

The Art of Seduction ☐
WI3 10 meters N46.4546 W86.5919

A typical climb along this stretch of the lakeshore trail. The wide formation and hanging daggers make for a challenging start and a strenuous lead. Climb the righthand side to gain the ramp where there is a tree to sling. Top out and belay from the cedar trees.

Calumet Girls ☐
WI3 9 meters
N46.4552 W86.5912

Slightly bulging, lots of fun and sometimes easy!

Ice Nine / Ice Ten ☐
WI3 3–10 meters N46.4556 W86.5907

A large variety of short, steep climbs form along the sandstone cliff for over a quarter of a mile.

LAKESHORE TRAIL

Sweet Mother Moses
WI4   23 meters   N46.4617 W86.5858

SMM is another Munising classic! Almost an exact replica of the *Dryer Hose*, a perfect vertical pillar ascends from the ice cone below and will challenge even the experienced climber. This climb forms in a distinct bowl, and is easy to spot from the trail above. After about a 2 mile walk from the parking lot, the trail takes a hard right turn before a small drainage right at the base of a huge cedar tree that is used as an excellent toprope anchor. If you want to get to the base, you can easily scramble down to the bottom of the cliff in a gully about 100 meters to the west of the climb.

Sweet Mother Moses
Liz Layne
Jon Jugenheimer

Sweet Mother Moses
Angela Vanwiemeersch ✗
Scott Crady 📷

LAKESHORE TRAIL

Giddy Up
✗ Joe Priebe
📷 Mike Wilkinson

Kemosabe ☐
WI4+   16 meters
N46.4657 W86.5824

Fifty feet right of *Hi Ho Silver*. Not quite as steep as its (neigh!)bor, but still thin at the bottom and sustained all the way up.

Hi Ho Silver ☐
WI6   20 meters
N46.4657 W86.5824

This skinny pillar forms climber's right of *Giddy Up*. It is an easy route to top rope with trees for anchors or else go for the lead with marginal gear.

Giddy Up ☐
WI3   25 meters   N46.4658 W86.5824

One of the easiest routes to find along the Lakeshore Trail. This climb is located in a large 90-degree corner in the cliff line. The set up is off the wooden bridge that crosses a large-volume creek. The fat pillar of ice is a five minute hike past *Sweet Mother Moses*.

A Man and a Horse ☐
WI4   13 meters   N46.4680 W86.5812

Located along the exposed cliff line climber's left of *Giddy Up*. It can be approached by carefully walking the steep cliff line to the northeast from *Giddy Up*, or rap in from above. This climb usually forms as a short, wide pillar and often features an adjoining dagger, which makes for interesting, three- dimensional climbing.

Mini Me ☐
WI3   7 meters
N46.4692 W86.5788

This climb is the first little drip you come across after walking east from *Hi Ho Silver*. The Lakeshore Trail goes right above it, but it is hard to see the actual climbing from the trail.

Sunny Day ☐
WI2   15 meters
N46.4694 W86.5786

This climb is only a few meters east of *Mini Me*, just another little dribble of water that freezes up every year. Unlike almost every climb in the park, *Sunny Day* is not vertical! One of the easiest climbs in Munising, it's a good place to practice leading before tackling one of the bigger climbs along the lakeshore.

A Man and A Horse
Mike Wilkinson ✕
Mike Wilkinson 📷

Turtle Power ☐
WI4   13 meters   N46.4703 W86.5776

Descend from the Lakeshore Trail in the bend where *Mini Me* and *Sunny Day* are found, but instead of going all the way to the lakeshore, carefully skirt around the cliffline to the northeast. It can be very steep in parts!

LAKESHORE TRAIL

HMR
Scott Bennett
Nic Dobbs

Many of the following climbs are situated along the cliff over Lake Superior. Climbing these can be an incredible thrill and an experience that is unique to the Upper Peninsula. That being said, it also creates a situation that can be potentially hazardous. If you lower into a climb over the water, you must be certain that you have the skills to get back out, either by climbing or ascending the rope.

Please Note: Miner's Castle Rd. is not plowed in the winter.

MINERS CASTLE

- THERE WILL BE MONSTERS
- KHIONE
- BOREAS
- HOT PEPPER WALL
- DEADWOOD
- RAPPIN' ICE
- LABYRINTH
- EL LANZON
- CURTAINS II
- PURPLE HAZE
- STRAWBERRY DAZE
- SPLIT LIP

LAKE SUPERIOR

- YOOPER GROOVE
- UDDER DELIGHT
- DAIRYLAND
- YELLOW CURTAINS
- MIDNIGHT RAMBLER
- LEFT SODA STRAW
- THE GOOD, THE BAD & THE UGLY
- THE CURTAIN CLIMB
- SUCK IT UP
- TURTLE POWER
- SUNNY DAY
- MINI ME

If the ice along the shore forms, climbers can walk or ski out Sand Point Bay, beginning from the end of Sand Point Road. If the shelf ice is not safe, take the Lakeshore Trail and rap in from above, making sure the climb has completely formed before doing so!

The climbs situated between *Dairyland* and Miners Castle are located along a very complex part of the Lakeshore Trail. The cliffline undulates between a vertical drop straight into the lake and large slopes of sandstone that separate the lake from the cliff and trail above. Depending on the season, a few of these climbs might not form, and in some banner years there is more ice than you could ever dream of. To access these spectacular climbs, it is much easier to travel and locate them from the frozen lake below if possible.

LAKESHORE TRAIL

Suck It Up ☐
WI4　　　25 meters
N46.4699 W86.5782

This route is hidden in the trees, but easily seen if you look to the west of *The Curtain Climb*. It forms as one of the four free-standing pillar routes between *Giddy Up* and *Dairyland*. Most easily accessed from the lakeshore after taking the access gully east of *Mini Me*.

Suck It Up
✗ Karsten Delap
📷 Mike Wilkinson

The Curtain Climb ☐
WI4　　　50 meters　　　N46.4709 W86.5761

This climb connects two curtains of ice. Start on the frozen lake ice and climb the lower pitch, which is about 5 meters of almost vertical ice followed by 25 to 30 meters of 30-degree snow slope to a vertical 10 meter final pitch. Multiple pitches and steep snow give this climb an alpine feel.

Curtain Climb & Suck It Up
📷 Mike Wilkinson

The Good, the Bad, and the Ugly
Mike Wilkinson

The Good, The Bad, and The Ugly
WI4   25 meters   N46.4716 W86.5746

This is one of the must do climbs in the area and will form in an average year by early January. This pillar is hard to see from above, can be a bit difficult to get to and set up a toprope anchor, but well worth the effort. Climb the hollow, vertical pillar, through a slightly overhanging section that provides the sting in the tail to make a great route. Just beware, this pillar is known to settle throughout the season and a scary looking horizontal fracture forms almost every year!

LAKESHORE TRAIL

The Good, the Bad, and the Ugly
Bill Thompson
Mario Molin

Left Soda Straw
WI4+   25 meters   N46.4723 W86.5733

This climb connects two curtains of ice. Start on the frozen lake ice and climb the lower pitch, which is about 5 meters of almost vertical ice followed by 25 to 30 meters of 30-degree snow slope to a vertical 10 meter final pitch. Multiple pitches and steep snow give this climb an alpine feel.

Midnight Rambler
Angela Limbach ✗
Doug Hemken 📷

Midnight Rambler ☐
WI4   25 meters
N46.4728 W86.5727

A fun, pumpy climb that is characteristic of the climbing in the Upper Peninsula. The topout can be a challenge as it tends to be overhung.

Yellow Curtains ☐
WI5   30 meters
N46.4755 W86.5698

Just around the corner, climber's right (west) of *Dairyland*. It doesn't always touch down, but when it does it's a long steep curtain of yellow colored ice. The ice usually gets smaller the closer to the ground it gets and spreads out on top, never getting all that thick.

LAKESHORE TRAIL

Dairyland
WI5　　　　　　　50 meters　　　　　　　N46.4758 W86.5692

This is it, the mother of all Munising climbs! Although it's not the hardest, it's the biggest, fattest, and most inspiring climb in the park. The climb usually forms in two HUGE pillars fed by a creek above, flanked at the top by massive bat wings. From the frozen lake to the top of the cliff, it is over 200 feet high, with 150 feet of actual climbing. The usual approach is to rappel down the climb from above and lead back out. If you are unable to climb back out to the top you have two options. If the lake is frozen, walk west towards the access gully by *Mini Me* and *Sunny Day* (about a 15 minute walk on the shelf ice). The other option is to jug the rappel line, have fun! So if you're out there, commit to it, this route will be on the top of your "ticked" list forever.

Dairyland
Mike Wilkinson

LAKESHORE TRAIL

Dairyland
Erik Olsen
Mike Wilkinson

Udder Delight
WI5   50 meters   N46.4764 W86.5684

The cliffline between *Dairyland* and *Yooper Groove* can host up to 6 climbs on a banner year. On an average year, *Udder Delight* usually comes in by February, and is the most striking of the lines in the area. A vertical pencil on the bottom opening up to a larger curtain of ice the higher you climb, this route screams "lead me!" Start on the lakeshore and set a belay at the bottom of the pillar. Ascend the pillar for an *Udder Delight*!

Dairyland
Colten Moore
Bryan DeAugustine

Yooper Groove
WI4   17 meters   N46.4780 W86.5665

Located about 500m east of *Dairyland*, this climb is almost impossible to find from above. When traveling on lake ice, pass *Dairyland*, then there is an area where the cliff line dives inward for about 50m and is not as vertical. This route is on the next outward bulge of the cliff line.

Dairyland is the large flow the shade, with the obvious thin pencil of ice in the background being Udder Delight.
Jon Jugenheimer

LAKESHORE TRAIL

Split Lip
WI5+ 55 meters
N46.4809 W86.5645

This route is a part of *Strawberry Daze*, a pillar that forms on the right side of the climb. It can be overhanging at the bottom and very small, sometimes only two feet thick and a foot wide.

Strawberry Daze
WI4+ 55 meters
N46.4811 W86.5644

Another bold and committing climb located northeast of *Dairyland*. The climb starts on the frozen shelf ice of Lake Superior and climbs a short first curtain to the large hanging curtain.

Strawberry Daze
2017 Michigan Ice Fest photo contest winner
Alex Schutzkus

Purple Haze ☐
WI4+ 55 meters
N46.4812 W86.5642

Purple Haze is the first formation to the east of *Strawberry Daze*. Start on the frozen lakeshore and ascend the easy 60-degree slope to the vertical ice above. Set up a belay here for the second pitch. The second pitch ascends up and left on a series of vertical pillars and steps to get on the hanging curtain above.

Curtains II ☐
WI3 60 meters
N46.4814 W86.5639

This "two" pitch climb is located just east of *Strawberry Daze* in a sandstone bowl. Start from the frozen lake shore on a 30-meter slab of ice and snow, climb he curtain to gain steeper ground. The upper curtain of ice is very reminiscent of *The Curtains* in the front country, but just a bit higher.

Dairyland
✕ James Loveridge
📷 Aaron Peterson

55

LAKESHORE TRAIL

El Lanzón ☐
WI4 20 meters N446.4819 W86.5631

This climb is tucked back into the trees on the upper vertical cliff band east of the *Strawberry Daze / Split Lip* formation. Wild three-dimensional ice structures can sometimes be found on this climb by the wind whipping up the dripping water. The route is blade-shaped, tall, narrow and deep like a knife, and reminded the first ascent party of the monolith in Chauvín, Peru named "El Lanzón" which means "the lance" in Spanish.

Labyrinth ☐
WI5 25 meters
N46.4821 W86.5628

Found just a bit east of the climb *El Lanzón*, *Labyrinth* is very similar in nature with sustained vertical ice columns.

El Lanzón
X Karsten Delap
📷 Mike Wilkinson

Rappin' Ice ☐
WI3 60 meters N46.4840 W86.5602

Farther east down the cliffline, *Rappin' Ice* is the last major climb before the dry walls west of Miners Castle. Climb up a 45+ meter WI2 to the WI3 upper crux. This climb is easiest to find from below, but if you are searching from above, find a large drainage about a 15 minute walk west of the Miners Castle overlook and descend.

Deadwood ☐
WI4+ 30 meters
N46.4844 W86.5597

A large, fat pillar of ice, that climbs like the standard Munising pillar to add to the list of pillars found in Munising. A long snow and ice cone leads to the vertical headwall into the trees above. A classic of the area.

Hot Pepper Wall ☐
WI3–4 18 meters
N46.4847 W86.5594

This wall consists of three separate lines. Left is *Banana Pepper*, middle is *Serrano Pepper* and the right is *Jalapeño Pepper*. These climbs, while short, are a touch spicy. All 3 start at the lake and end halfway up on a tree covered terrace.

Boreas ☐
WI4 20 meters
N46.4852 W86.5589

Khione ☐
WI4 20 meters
N46.4852 W86.5588

Located very close to one another, *Boreas* and *Khione* are about a 10–15 minute walk west from the Miners Castle overlook. They can be found from above as a series of small dendritic drainages that flow into two distinct points on the cliffline. Or, they can be found from below by walking back from Miners Castle and looking up high into the trees. They are shorter vertical curtains of ice that can be a fun toprope or a lead depending on how thick the curtains form.

Boreas
X Erik Olsen
📷 Mike Wilkinson

There Will Be Monsters ☐
WI4 20 meters N6.4858 W86.5587

To find this climb you have two options, with the easier from the lake ice below, by looking along the high cliffline just east of *Boreas* and *Khione*. From above, when the lake ice is not in, a shorter approach is to walk about 10 minutes east from Miners Castle down the Lakeshore Trail to where two small wooden bridges are located. Follow the drainage down from the second bridge to access the climb. *There Will Be Monsters* usually forms as two distinct lines, with the flow on climber's left being the easier of the two. Stem your way up vertical terrain until the angle begins to ease off, and hopefully you are not frightened along the way.

MINERS TO MOSQUITO

Conrad Anker
Karsten Delap

MINERS BEACH TO MOSQUITO BEACH
7 ROUTES • WI3–4 • 10–55m

The ice located between Miners Beach and Mosquito Beach is fantastic for the novice "over the lake climber," or for one who wants to the experience the solitude of the north woods in winter. *Bridalveil Falls*, the gem of this area, is usually the first climb to form in Pictured Rocks National Lakeshore. Climbing above the open waters of the largest lake in the world is certainly a test of your mental fortitude. Located close to Miners Beach is the popular learning area of *Potato Patch Falls*, with *Bridalveil Falls* located just a 30-minute walk further east along the lakeshore. An easy snowmobile approach, or a long ski down Miners Castle Road, make this area great for an overnight mission, or a simple day trip to climb multiple routes before heading back home.

To access this area, ski or snowmobile Miners Castle Road from the intersection of Carmody and Miners Road (where the plow stops) until the first Y in the road at the top of the big hill. Take a right at the Y, and proceed downhill and over the Miners River before a long straightaway to a T intersection. Take a right at the T and travel to the end of the road and summer trailhead (four miles to this point). Walk up the Lakeshore Trail for less than a quarter of a mile to the cliff band and take a left at the base of it to access *Potato Patch Falls*, whereas to access *Bridalveil Falls*, stay on the Lakeshore Trail to the top of the cliff band and follow the trail (if one is broken) for just over a half mile to the obvious creek that feeds the climb.

MINERS TO MOSQUITO

Sunset at Miner's Beach — Mike Wilkinson

Potato Patch Falls
WI3   10 meters
N46.4989 W86.5302

A fantastic warmup climb, *Potato Patch Falls* is formed from a creek that runs just past the Potato Patch campground that is located on top of the cliff. The approach is easy from the trailhead (once there) and takes about 10 minutes. Start at the end of the road, on the east side of Miners Beach where the large wooden sign for the Lakeshore Trailhead is located. Walk up the trail until you see the cliffline trending north/south with the trail cutting a path between them. Leave the trail at the base of the cliff and head climber's left to the bottom of the climb, or continue up the hill to access the large trees used for toprope anchors.

Bridalveil Falls — Stephanie Moore / Mike Wilkinson

Flaming Stink Socks
WI3   10 meters
N46.4987 W86.5308

Located in the same bowl as *Potato Patch Falls*, this is the right side of the wall and not fed directly from the creek.

Potato Patch Falls — Braeden Hyland / Matt Abbotts

The Wall
WI4–5   10–50 meters   N46.5023 W86.5288

When hiking the Lakeshore Trail above or the frozen lake below, *The Wall* is a large bowl containing up to 15 independent lines on a good year. Just a 10-minute walk past *Potato Patch Falls*, some of these lines form only near the bottom of the cliff while others form at the top of the cliff with only rock below.

The Rim
WI4–5   10–50 meters   N46.5050 W86.5240

The Rim is like *The Wall*, but the vertical top of the cliff and vertical bottom of the cliff is separated by a sloping ledge covered in trees. Most everyone climbs the vertical section at the top of the cliff as it is the easiest to find from above, and climb back out, but note some lines go all the way to the water below. Like *The Wall*, *The Rim* is also found in a large bowl with up to 15 independent lines forming on any given year.

Class on Bridalveil Falls During Ice Fest 2017
✕ Roman Zinov
📷 Mike Wilkinson

MINERS TO MOSQUITO

Bridalveil Falls
WI3   60 meters   N46.5085 W86.5233

Bridalveil Falls is the perfect spot to experience climbing over open water for the first time, so don't have cold feet about it, take your vows and lower in! About a 30-minute walk east past *Potato Patch Falls* on the Lakeshore Trail, cross a short wooden bridge with a swamp to your right and the creek flowing under the bridge below your feet. Immediately follow the creek bed towards the lake to find the climb cascading off the cliff and into the lake below. Starting as a shallow ramp from Lake Superior, the climb becomes steeper with a few body lengths of vertical ice to finish the route to the top of the cliff.

Note: West of Mosquito Beach, and East of *Road to Nowhere* there are up to another dozen small daggers (on a good year) that do not top out on the cliff. They can usually be climbed, then rappelled back to the frozen lake via V threads. None of them are named, as the zone forms differently every season.

Left at the Altar ☐
WI4   30 meters
N46.5085 W86.5233

More of a variation of *Bridalveil Falls* than a route of its own, climb the steep spray ice to the left of *Bridalveil Falls*, through small umbrellas and candle drip features and top out above and left of Bridalveil.

Road to Nowhere ☐
WI4   60+ meters
N46.5105 W86.5203

Five minutes past *Bridalveil Falls* is another large bowl like *The Wall*, but rarely do any of the routes top out. The climb is best approached late in the season on the frozen lake ice. Pick from the multiple lines of ascent and rappel back to the lake via V threads.

Bridalveil Falls
Joe Thill
Scott Crady

MOSQUITO TO CHAPEL

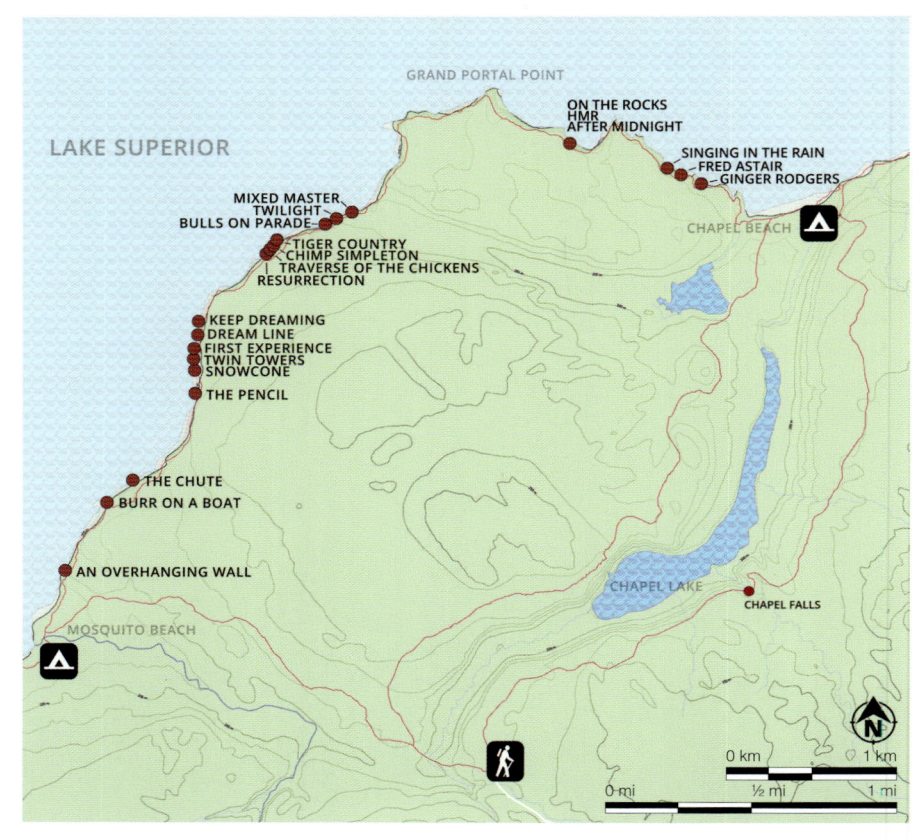

Map labels (Lake Superior side, north to south):
- GRAND PORTAL POINT
- ON THE ROCKS
- HMR
- AFTER MIDNIGHT
- SINGING IN THE RAIN
- FRED ASTAIR
- GINGER RODGERS
- CHAPEL BEACH
- MIXED MASTER
- TWILIGHT
- BULLS ON PARADE
- TIGER COUNTRY
- CHIMP SIMPLETON
- TRAVERSE OF THE CHICKENS
- RESURRECTION
- KEEP DREAMING
- DREAM LINE
- FIRST EXPERIENCE
- TWIN TOWERS
- SNOWCONE
- THE PENCIL
- THE CHUTE
- BURR ON A BOAT
- AN OVERHANGING WALL
- MOSQUITO BEACH
- CHAPEL LAKE
- CHAPEL FALLS

MOSQUITO BEACH TO CHAPEL BEACH
22 ROUTES • WI3–6 • 20–60m

From left to right; Keep Dreaming, Dream Line, First Experience, Twin Towers, Snow Cone and The Pencil just out of view. Twin Towers is the largest flow right of the large cave, and Snow Cone is slightly behind the large rock tower.
📷 Jon Jugenheimer

The heart of the backcountry ice climbing in Munising is located here. This four-mile stretch of rock, ice, lake and forest is located between the beaches of Mosquito and Chapel. It can provide an experience unlike anywhere else on the main land. Two hundred foot colorful sandstone sea cliffs, rope-stretching climbs, and an unblocked view north into the cold waters of Lake Superior are abundant here, especially standing on top of Grand Portal Point! While this area holds some of the most sought-after climbs in the region, and one climb (*HMR*) that is a top 10 ice climb in North America, it is also the hardest to get to in the park, and requires commitment, perseverance and a solid Yooper "sisu" attitude!

To get here, drive to the town of Melstrand, 15 miles east of Munising on Hwy H58. Turn left (north) on Chapel Road and drive for two miles to a fork in the road. This is where the directions will change from year to year based on the winter logging activity in the area. If logging operations are not in progress, the road will not be plowed and you must park your vehicle here, well to the side of the road for continued snowmobile access. If the road is plowed, continue down the right fork (NPS sign) for a half-mile to a left at the next fork (the right fork is usually not plowed) and continue for another 1.5 miles. This has historically been the area where there has been a parking lot plowed out for climbers to park (courtesy of the logging company), or else park at the end of the plowed road well out of the way of any of the roads (plowed or not), any logging machinery or logging infrastructure. From this point, it is just under a mile to the summer time Chapel Beach Trailhead. There you can head left to Mosquito Beach or right to Chapel Beach via their respective trails.

The climbs in this chapter are described west to east, from Mosquito to Chapel. To get to Mosquito beach, take the Mosquito trail for 2 miles and, unlike in July, you don't need to bring DEET.

Note: the quickest access to *HMR* is by first taking the Mosquito Beach Trail down the hill and over the Chapel Creek bridge. Take your first (and only) right onto the secondary Chapel Beach trail to the Beach. This trail will save approximately half a mile from using the main Chapel Beach trail that passes over Chapel Falls.

MOSQUITO TO CHAPEL

An Overhanging Wall ☐
WI4–6   20 meters
N46.5296 W86.4915

This climb is overhanging the whole way, and gets steeper the higher you climb. The route forms by the spray from the lake freezing on the wall plus water seeping through the rock. The ice doesn't get very thick, so it is best done as a toprope when the lake ice is solid. The climb is only a few hundred feet northeast of Mosquito Beach, which is an ideal vantage point to assess the conditions.

Burr On A Boat ☐
WI3   25 meters
N46.5330 W86.4887

Located just east of the "Lovers Leap Arch," this climb also forms from a combination of spray ice and seeping groundwater. The windblown spray can create wild ice formations that will challenge your ascent. You can easily spot this climb from the east looking back west along the lake, or along the lakeshore trail above where the trees are often heavily coated in ice.

An Overhanging Wall
X Peter Vintoniv
📷 Andrew Burr

The Chute ☐
WI3   20 meters   N46.5341 W86.4869

About 100 meters east of *Burr on a Boat* an iced-up gully extends from the lake to the top of the cliff forming one of the easier climbs in the region. The lake doesn't always freeze solid here, and is best scoped from above the climb *Twin Towers* to check conditions before rappelling in.

The Pencil ☐
WI6   40 meters
N46.5387 W86.4825

A svelte pillar of white ice originating high in the cliff band, becoming ever smaller as it barely touches the lake. Rarely forming, this sketchy column of ice above the crashing waves or the frozen lake both makes you want to climb it and run away at the same time.

Snow Cone ☐
WI3+   40 meters
N46.5403 W86.4827

Easy to find by looking for the prominent rock tower just a few meters west of the climb. *Snow Cone* starts off vertical, then backs off near the top. There are plenty of trees to set up a toprope and a shelf of lake ice usually forms making a bottom belay possible. This route reliably forms each year as it isn't a vertical pillar, but rather a seepage making a sheet of ice.

Twin Towers
Jackson Marvel X
Jon Jugenheimer 📷

MOSQUITO TO CHAPEL

Twin Towers
WI4+   45 meters   N46.5399 W86.4826

These two columns begin separately, but merge into one large curtain at the top. Start off the frozen shelf ice and climb 20 meters of vertical ice, gunning for the halfway ledge above the columns to shake out. The last 25 meters is a mix of vertical and lower-angle ice to the trees above, finishing just 50 meters east of *Snow Cone*. This is the classic climb in the Mosquito Beach area and not to be missed.

Twin Towers
Ben Erdmann
Mike Wilkinson

First Experience
WI5 45 meters N46.5406 W86.4824

Fifteen meters left of *Twin Towers*, *First Experience* forms as a thin pillar, or sometimes not at all, to make this the most challenging climb of the three that are all next to each other. Sometimes no wider than a body width, this vertical pillar of ice doesn't always touch, but when it does it is a challenge just to get off the ground.

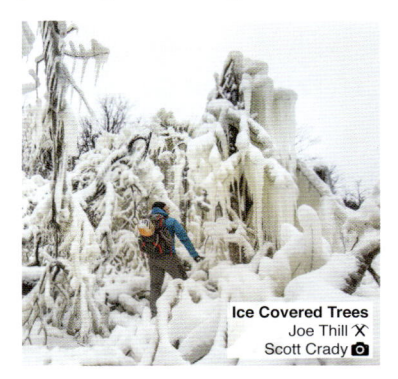

Ice Covered Trees
Joe Thill X
Scott Crady 📷

Dream Line
WI5 45 meters N46.5412 W86.4821

Just to the east of Rainbow Cave (large cave east of *Twin Towers*) this whisper of ice beckons to be climbed, but rarely ever is. Almost impossible to find directly from above, this climb needs the lake to freeze for the approach and to support the column. Rarely do these perfect conditions occur, but when they do make sure you take advantage of them!

Keep Dreaming
WI5 45 meters N46.5418 W86.4821

Keep Dreaming is found left (east) of the Rainbow Cave in the next smaller cave. If formed, as it rarely does, it is a collection of thin pencils dripping off the lip, sometimes welded together, sometimes not, finishing with an ice ramp above to the trees. Technical climbing is the game here on any given year as the abstract thought of this climb is usually stronger than the actual ice forming it.

Twin Towers
X Nic Dobbs
📷 Aaron Peterson

MOSQUITO TO CHAPEL

Note on the next four climbs: They are columns of ice only attached to the sandstone cliff, and pretty much nothing else until the lake is frozen below. The vertical sandstone cliff goes straight into the lake for another 15 meters thus there is no grounding of the ice to support its own weight like on land. Without a large ice shelf below the climbs, it is recommended to stay off as they have been known to spontaneously collapse or the shelf ice move with heavy wave action generated by a strong north west wind.

Chimp Simpleton
X Angela Vanwiemeersch
📷 Jon Jugenheimer

Resurrection ☐
WI6   35 meters
N46.5452 W86.47748

Originally climbed as a re-formed column with a large roof at the fracture line, *Resurrection* will bring you back to life once you ascend from the lake back to the forest above. A large, beautiful yellow, white and blue column of ice both attached to the cliff and the frozen shelf ice below. Rarely another column will form just 5 meters to the right of *Resurrection*, but it is unnamed in this book.

Traverse of the Chickens ☐
WI4   50 meters
N46.5454 W86.4772

This interesting traverse looks harder than it is, and climbs better than it locks! The route starts just a few meters left of *Resurrection* and ascends a vertical bulge of ice for 10 meters. On top of the bulge climb the long upward left ramp covered in ice to the crux moves of getting on to the top of the typically unformed and unnamed pillar. Climb the last 10 meters of the ice to the trees above.

Resurrection Area
📷 Mike Wilkinson

The fallen pillar behind the airboat is Resurrection, with the Traverse of the Chickens trending up and left to the hanger above.
Keith Ladzinski

Chimp Simpleton
WI5   30 meters
N46.5455 W86.4770

Chimp Simpleton is just that, so simple a chimp could climb it. The most straightforward climbing in this zone, pick the side of the column of ice that looks best to you and swing and kick your way to the top. Located anywhere else there would be a line on this climb all day long, located where it is, you may be the only person all season long to have climbed it.

Tiger Country
WI6   35 meters
N46.5459 W86.4768

A BASE jumping term for where not to land, *Tiger Country* is just that, don't fall. The route starts with thin, sublimated ice that grows thicker as you climb to an actual column of ice strong enough to get to the trees above. This wild climb, when formed in its original condition, is one of the wildest ice leads in the park.

MOSQUITO TO CHAPEL

Bulls on Parade
Jackson Marvell
Jon Jugenheimer

Bulls On Parade ☐
WI4   40 meters   N46.5466 W86.4734

Bulls on Parade is easy to find as there is a wooden bridge crossing a small creek, which is the only bridge in this zone before you get to the western rock wall of Grand Portal Point. There is also a large sandstone "fin" at the bottom of the route that is easily recognizable. Walk towards the lake from the trail, bashing your way through thick brush and pick a point to rappel down. You will most likely not know if the route is fully formed until you are over the edge, but there is a good chance that it is, as there is a flowing water source. The climb starts with a short vertical step which ramps off for 10 meters. Ever steepening ice leads to a vertical exit, where otherworldly bat wings and umbrellas form to climber's right.

Twilight ☐
WI4+   40 meters   N46.5471 W86.4726

Twilight doesn't form every year, but when it does, its golden yellow vertical pillar of ice is classic to the region. The crux is short, but the whole climb packs a punch.

Mixed Master ☐
WI4+   40 meters   N46.5471 W86.4726

Not too far around the corner (east) from *Bulls on Parade*, *Mixed Master* is located in a very shallow, open book that doesn't always form every year. Climb the white and yellow daggers, connecting them together if the curtain isn't welded together. Note, the climb doesn't always form to the lip, which keeps life interesting when trying to top out.

MOSQUITO TO CHAPEL

HMR
WI5   60 meters   N46.5508 W86.4566

Perhaps one of the most scenic and sought-after routes in the Lake Superior basin. *HMR* is 60 meters of steep and sustained ice, directly above either an open sea or a frozen surface with the crux of the route sometimes just being able leave the belay where the old spray ice was undercut and washed away by the crashing waves when the lake was still open.

When the lake is frozen, it is best approached from Chapel Beach, walking the frozen moonscape surface, only to round the final corner and have your mind blown by this awesome site.

When the lake is not frozen, simply approach from the top via the Lakeshore Trail from the beach to find the climb and either top belay or rappel in to lead back out!

HMR in a year when the left and right variations did not form
Jon Jugenheimer
Aaron Peterson

On the Rocks
WI6   60 meters   N46.5508 W86.4566

This right variation of *HMR* ascends the spray and pencil-like pillar feature connecting the ice through an upper small roof. Long runouts and stubby screws were reported during the 2017 Ice Fest. Ice blobs, thin sticks and good luck are all you have from the belay for the first 25–30 meters to a vertical pillar (crux) to the short headwall above where good screws are finally found in the thicker ice. *On the Rocks* is a very serious route, possibly the most "out there" found in the entire lakeshore.

After Midnight
WI5+   60 meters
N46.5508 W86.4566

This line far to the left of the main flow of *HMR*, starts above the high water mark and ascends the sheet of ice at its thickest point to finish in the trees well left of the standard finish of *HMR*.

MOSQUITO TO CHAPEL

Singing In the Rain ☐
WI3   30 meters
N46.5494 W86.4498

Found in the furthest bowl from the beach, *Singing In The Rain* is common to the other climbs in the area in which you will rap in and climb out on a vertical ice section that eases off at the top.

Fred Astaire ☐
WI3   30 meters
N46.5491 W86.4489

"I just put my feet in the air and move them around. The higher up you go, the more mistakes you are allowed. Right at the top, if you make enough of them, it's considered to be your style" ~ Fred Astaire

Rap to the lake ice, or to a shelf above the open water, and, like Fred, dance above the waves.

Singing In the Rain Area
Angela Vanwiemeersch X
Mike Wilkinson 📷

The Singing In The Rain Area is a series of bowls between HMR and Chapel Beach. When the lake is not frozen, the white ice and snow above stand in stark contrast to the turquoise waters below. The name is a tip of the helmet to Paul Kuenn, an early pioneer of the area. Back in the 1980s Paul skied out to the Grand Portal Point Area, and with one wooden piolet and one short tool, led a long sustained climb. It was a wet, late March ascent so he called the climb Singing In the Rain. True to Paul's character the ascent was never really recorded. In 2013 that route was unknowingly renamed HMR after a now infamous ice fest party, but the legend of PK's original name lives on in these three neighboring climbs.

Ginger Rodgers ☐
WI3   30 meters   N46.5487 W86.4475

"The only way to enjoy anything in this life is to earn it first." ~ Ginger Rodgers

And earn it you will! With a long approach this climb is usually something to tick off while out visiting the *HMR* area. Spend the night at the Chapel Beach area for the full experience! This is the closest climb to Chapel Beach, about a 10-minute ski from the wooden bridge on the far western side of the beach.

CHAPEL EAST

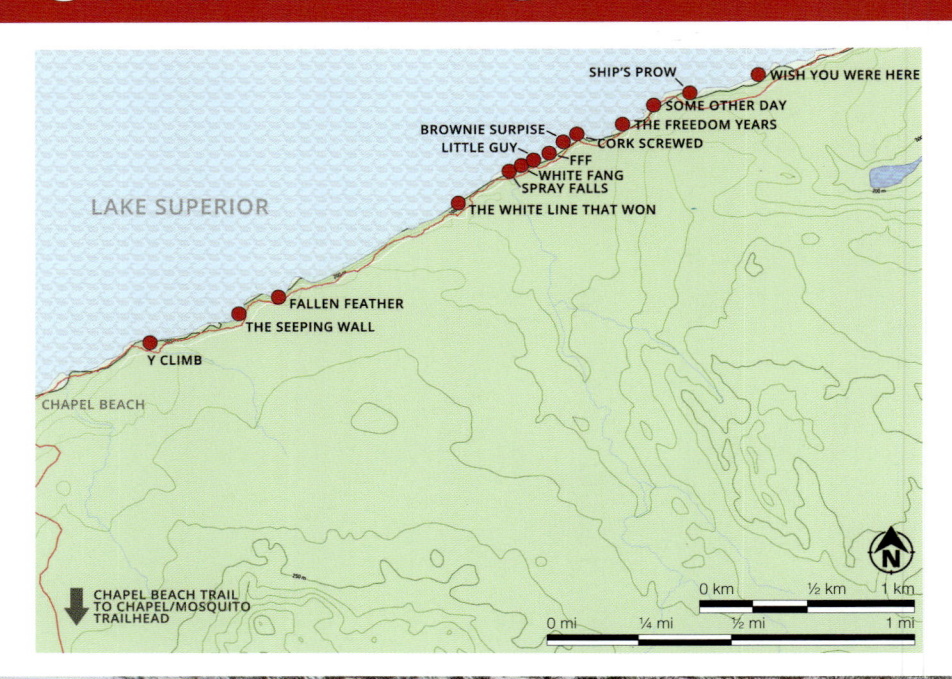

Fallen Feather
Sam Elias
Mike Wilkinson

CHAPEL BEACH EAST 14 ROUTES • WI3–6 • 10–50m

The climbs east of Chapel Beach are the furthest from the car in PRNL requiring hard work to get there, but the potential for amazing ice is well worth the slog that it can take, even after a big snowfall. The climbs develop over and into the lake and come into condition on a normal year by late December/January, with the shelf ice soon thereafter, usually by early February at the latest. Since these climbs drop directly into the lake, a good pack of shelf ice is highly useful to walk on. Once the shelf ice develops, it remains for some time as the cliffline is north-facing and will not see the sun's rays until the end of March. If you climb here, bring a big puffy as there is nothing to stop the north winds blowing across the lake from Canada.

The access to this area is by snowshoeing or skiing three plus miles from the parking area to Chapel Beach (see the description for Grand Portal Point page 65). This climbing area starts at Chapel Beach and goes east for approximately two and a half miles until the end of the cliffline. The climbs here range in height from 10 to 50 meters and range in difficulty from WI3 to WI6. This area is not a destination for beginners, as most of the climbs are WI4 or harder.

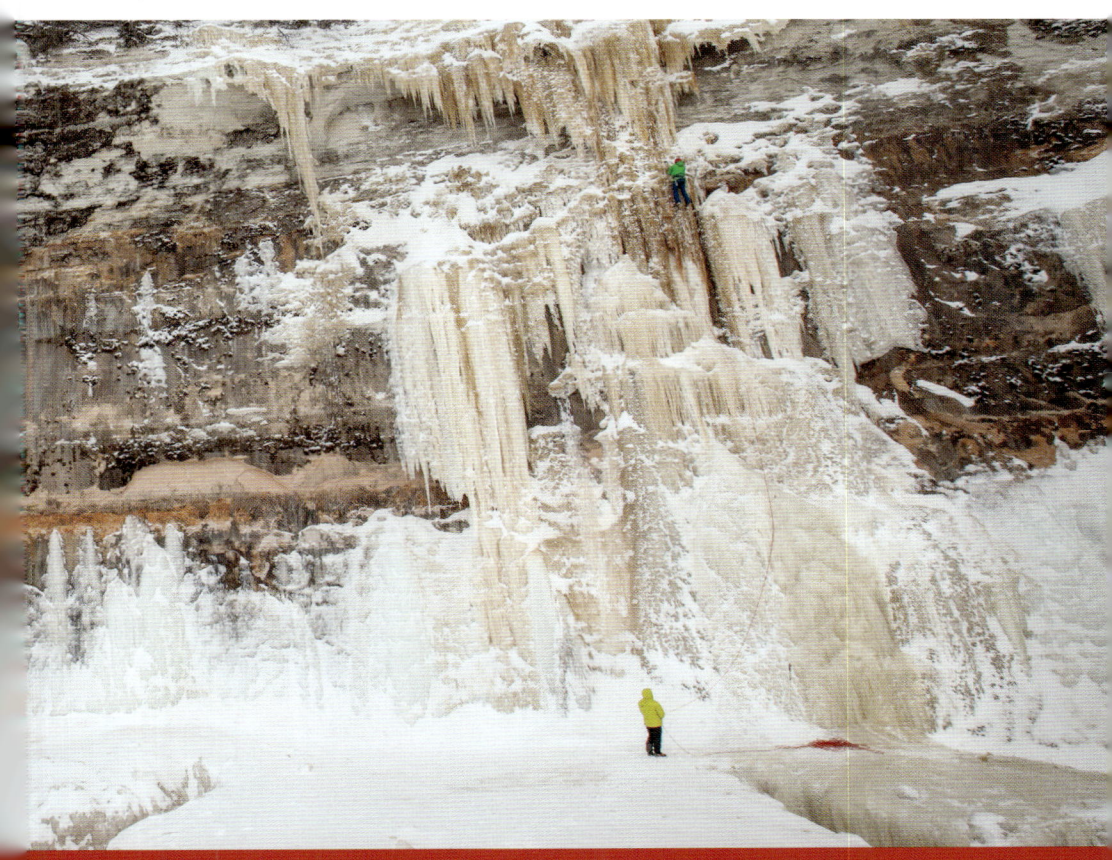

CHAPEL EAST

Scoping out the Lakeshore
Mike Wilkinson

Y Climb
WI3   10 meters   N46.5509 W86.4310

The first named climb east of Chapel Rock, just a short 10–15 minutes from the beach depending on your mode of travel and the snow pack. This climb is easily identified from above as two deep stream beds merge together to form a Y, with two wooden bridges over each tributary set back from the cliff edge. The two streams are usually wet year-round which makes this climb form every year, but also can make for wet climbing almost all year. This is a great warm up climb for the area and also offers easy access to the lake ice below if frozen.

Seeping Wall
WI5   30 meters   N46.5521 W86.4258

The *Seeping Wall* is just that, seeping ground water slowly freezing as it oozes out of the soft earth. Knowing how slowly it is fed, and the length of the overhanging drop to the lake below, this climb rarely forms and is known as a "once every 20 years climb" Thus, if it is in, which it rarely ever is, this is one not to miss. Located east of *Y Climb*, it is the first, and the largest of the large bowls in this area and easily seen from above while traveling towards *Spray Falls*.

Fallen Feather
WI5+   25 meters
N46.5527 W86.4237

A thin continuous dribble of a snot-cicle forming from the lip to the cold water below. This "climb" when formed provides one of the most entertaining and thought provoking ascents along the entire lakeshore. Climber beware, this is one BOLD ascent!

Fallen Feather
Sam Elias
Mike Wilkinson

CHAPEL EAST

The White Line that Won ☐
WI4   28 meters   N46.5565 W86.4135

The White Line comes into shape about once every five years or so, and sometimes has a neighbor just to the left (unnamed). This climb, when formed is located roughly a ¼ mile west of *Spray Falls*, and is easiest found via walking west on the frozen lake from *Spray Falls*. The climb is very easy to spot, as it is usually the only, and the largest piece of ice between *Spray Falls* and *Fallen Feather*.

Spray Falls
Jon Jugenheimer

Spray Falls ☐
WI3   20 meters
N46.5579 W86.4105

A great climb, which everyone should do at least once! Every year this route seems to form a bit differently. This may be due to the high volume of water coming off the top, fed by Spray Creek.

Walk east from Chapel Beach for about 30-45 minutes along the Lakeshore Trail, allowing more time if the trail isn't broken. After some small hills, cross a wooden bridge over the large creek that feeds *Spray Falls*.

White Fang ☐
WI6   20 meters
N46.5580 W86.4100

The first dagger of ice located east of *Spray Falls*. This climb is usually thin, technical and challenging but at least its short!

Little Guy ☐
WI3   20 meters
N46.5579 W86.4095

Just to the east of *White Fang* is *Little Guy*, a pillar of ice with a water tube in the middle.

Unlike most Munising climbs, it slopes back at the top, getting easier as you climb higher.

FFF ☐
WI4   24 meters   N46.5585 W86.4086

A few meters to the right of *Brownie Surprise* a pillar sometimes forms on banner seasons to offer a bonus climb in the area! Start on a pillar of ice leading to a widening curtain to top out finishing with a tree root and a dirt stick. *FFF* is a fun climb, with nothing to fear.

Little Guy
X Gina Vendola
📷 Jon Jugenheimer

Brownie Surprise
WI4   24 meters   N46.5579 W86.4076

A short but vertical curtain of ice. You can belay from the top in a bunch of trees, as well as toprope from them. But just a note, it's extremely thick at the top which makes the setup tricky.

FFF
Gina Vendola
Jon Jugenheimer

Cork Screwed
WI4-   15 meters
N46.5592 W86.4070

Tucked away in a corner, just below the *Spray Falls* lookout that is on top of the cliff, this wild for Munising climb snakes its way up cracks and corners to where the ice pours out from the sandstone rock walls. Climb as far as you can make it off the deck, then rappel from a V-thread back down. Note: The ice has never been witnessed to go all the way to the top of the cliff.

The Freedom Years
WI4–5   15–45 meters
N46.5580 W86.4076

On an average year a few climbs form here, on a banner year this is a collection of a half dozen plus drips, daggers, curtains, pillars and seeps. No one particular climb forms the same season after season, but rather this zone of awesomeness can be a new playground for you year after year.

CHAPEL EAST

Some Other Day
WI4 40+ meters N46.5599 W86.4027

Located deep in an inside corner, just east of a deep cave, this classic is seldom climbed as it is near the end of a long journey from the trailhead. Sometimes forming as two separate pillars joined at the top where the slope rolls back to less than vertical, sometimes forming as a wide sheet of ice, today is always the day to climb *Some Other Day*.

Ship's Prow
Jon Jugenheimer

The Ship's Prow ☐
WI4   25 meters
N46.5609 W86.4006

Walk past *Some Other Day* on the frozen lake, through an arch and look left. Just like the prow of a ship, this steep climb forms on the blunt rock face protecting the arch from the strong north winds, and giving you safe passage traversing up and left, up and left to the birch trees above.

Wish You Were Here ☐
WI5   25 meters   N46.5617 W86.3966

Located at the very end of the line, as far as anyone needs to travel from the thoughts of past partnerships and how you wish them here with you today. Dealer's choice, climb either the right or the left pillar to the headwall above, on your arms the whole way. Descent is from a V thread at the top of the ice headwall, as the ice usually doesn't go all the way to the dead tree above.

Wish You Were Here
Rafael Slawinski
Jon Jugenheimer

INLAND CLIMBS

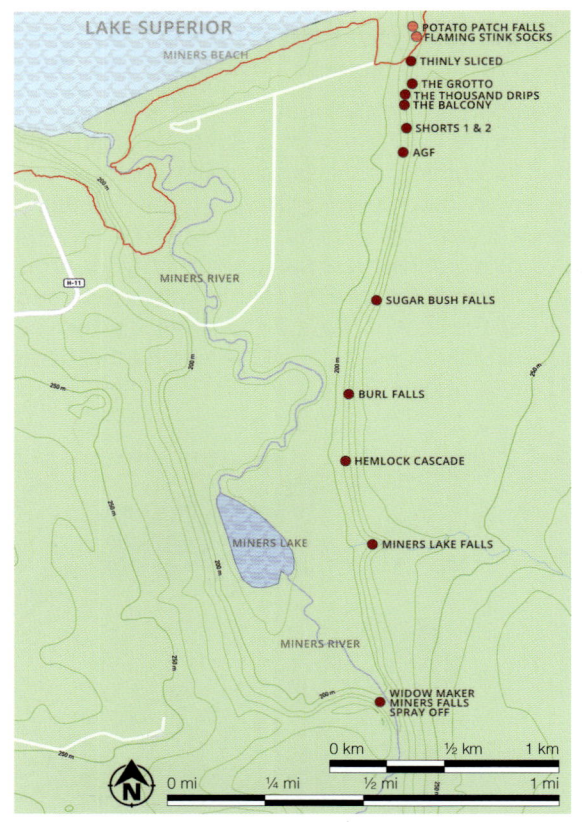

INLAND CLIMBS
11 ROUTES
WI2–4 • 5–30m

Isolated in the deep woods of the National Lakeshore, the Inland Climbs Area lives all by itself offering adventurous climbers the opportunity to ascend routes that are seldom climbed. Similar to other climbing areas located by the lake, these climbs can be a long slog to get to. Rest assured you will have the climbs to yourself! To access these climbs, grab your pack, strap on the skis and get ready to put some kilometers on.

Miners Lake Falls
Mike Wilkinson
Mike Wilkinson

Miners Falls
Mike Wilkinson
Mike Wilkinson

Sometimes the approach is half the fun
Jack Frost

INLAND CLIMBS

To access these climbs, drive north on Miners Castle Road until the plow stops at the intersection of Carmody Road. Park here and head north via ski, snowshoe or snowmobile (see page 58 for detailed directions (Miners–Mosquito section). When you reach Miner's Beach head east on the Lakeshore Trail. Hike up the trail until you reach a sandstone bluff that bisects the trail. Head off the established trail to the climber's right (south), and walk along the bluff to find the base of the climbs.

Miners Lake Falls and *Miners Falls* are located to the south along this same sandstone ridge.

Thinly Sliced ☐
WI3   7 meters
N46.4979 W86.5304

Be delicate on this thin smear located on the sandstone bluff right off of the Lakeshore Trail.

The Grotto ☐
WI3   6 meters
N46.4969 W86.5303

A small sandstone bowl that has a vertical sheet of ice and a lower-angle ramp to climber's right.

Thousand Drips ☐
WI3   5 meters
N46.4965 W86.5306

A very short but wide sheet of ice suitable for beginners to practice skills.

The Balcony ☐
WI3   7 meters
N46.4962 W86.5307

This short climb has two sections divided by a sidewalk-sized balcony.

Shorts One & Two ☐
WI3   5 meters
N46.4953 W86.5306

Two very short vertical sections of ice situated side by side.

AGF ☐
WI4   20 meters
N46.4945 W86.5307

AGF is the largest pillar in this section. Located in a sandstone bowl, the climb forms a typical vertical pillar.

Burl Falls ☐
WI4   13 meters
N46.4858 W86.5335

The second-highest route along this ridge, it offers a playful pillar.

Thinly Sliced
✗ Linda Wappner
📷 Bill Thompson

AGF
Angela Vanwiemeersch
Jon Jugenheimer

Sugar Bush Falls
WI4 20 meters
N46.4891 W86.5321

If you're climbing this climb you are a hardy soul! Located in a very remote section of the park, it's a long way to go and a short climb once you get there.

Hemlock Cascade
WI3 9 meters
N46.4835 W86.5336

Nestled in a conifer forest one will find solitude on this short cascading falls.

INLAND CLIMBS

Miners Falls
WI3   10 meters
N46.4748 W86.5319

Ski approximately 2 miles down Miners Castle Road until you see the sign for *Miners Falls*, turn right (east) and head to the end of the road. The falls are about 1.5 miles from Miners Castle Road. The falls only freeze after sustained cold weather due to their high volume of water flow.

Widow Maker
WI3   10 meters
N46.4748 W86.5319

Climbers left of *Miners Falls*, this short but stout climb begins with a wide apron and narrows to a difficult finish.

Spray Off
WI4   10 meters
N46.4748 W86.5319

Located on the wall to climber's right of *Miners Falls*, the climb forms when spray from the waterfall hits the wall, covering it in blobs of somewhat unstable ice.

Spray Off
Bill Thompson
Bill Thompson

Miners Falls
Unknown
Michael Tokarz

Widow Maker
Bill Thompson
Bill Thompson

Miners Lake Falls
WI3   18 meters
N46.4805 W86.5323

A pillar on the east side of Miners Lake that forms up just like *The Dryer Hose*. From the trail heading to *Miners Falls* go north down the hill onto the lake. If frozen, cross the lake, if not, walk around the lake (very thick brush) to the center of the east side of the lake. Unlike the rest of the cliff line, thick pine trees surround the falls so you cannot see the climb from across the lake or from the viewing platform at *Miners Falls*.

Chapel Falls
WI2   30 meters
N46.5287 W86.4441

If you're looking for a long, low-angle climb this is it! Be warned: If it is a high snow year the climb will be buried. Head to Melstrand (see description for Grand Portal Point) and proceed to the Chapel Beach trailhead. Take the path (east) heading towards Chapel Beach for about a mile or so, the falls will be on your left, with a wooden viewing platform above. As a side note, the cliffline to your left on the approach sometimes has short sections of ice on it, not a destination, but rather a distraction. This is another higher volume river and is slow to form up.

GRAND ISLAND

West Shore Curtains
Adam Dailey
Aaron Peterson

Grand Island is the forbidden fruit of Michigan ice climbing, It's always good, it's always right there, and often we're just not able to have it. It is the most remote, the hardest to access and arguably the best ice climbing in the Midwest.

Sitting just a mile offshore in Munising Bay, this frozen playground is as good as it gets. The island is about 25 miles around and virtually all of the shoreline is plastered with ice just begging to be climbed. We've broken the island into four zones, the East Channel, Trout Bay, the West Shore and the North Shore. It contains over 80 named routes and many more opportunities for a first experience.

The most dangerous part of climbing on Grand Island is getting to Grand Island. Solid lake ice does not form every year and lake ice conditions vary throughout the season with the penalty for an accident being very high. We are including information in each section with the best and safest way to access the area, please heed this advice. We also suggest calling the National Park Service before you head out for the most up-to-date reports on lake ice conditions.

EAST CHANNEL

Crossing the East Channel
📷 Mike Wilkinson

EAST CHANNEL ∞ ROUTES • WI2–6 • 30–80m

The East Channel of Grand Island is the bread and butter of the island, and where most climbers spend their time once the lake is safe to cross. Easily seen from Sand Point Road, the East Channel would hold hundreds of "separately" named climbs if it were in Colorado, but since it isn't and it's really just a wall of ice, we call it another set of curtains! The approach from the Sand Point parking lot is about a mile from the beach to the first climbable ice, with the width of the climbing area almost being the same distance along the island. The typical approach is walking, but many people use snowshoes after a storm, skis for the fastest human powered travel and snowmobiles for the quickest access. A boat has also been used in the past by a few more adventurous and slightly crazy individuals.

The climbing ranges from great beginner ice, all the way to fun climbs for seasoned professionals. There are curtains, pillars, caves to discover, and both short and long climbs to be found. The only thing that is missing is easy access to the top of the climbs. On most every climb one must lead to get the rope up, so keep that in mind when planning your trip across the channel.

The *East Channel Curtains* are usually climbable by the first of the year, but the challenge is getting there. The National Park Service regularly issues warnings in the early season for thin ice and advises against travel for good measure. The channel holds a fast current, especially where the permanent marker buoy is located, and the ice could be less than an inch thick even when ice in Munising Bay is over a foot thick. Only you can make the decision to head out to the East Channel, but when you do, make sure the lake is well frozen. We suggest calling the Park Service for a conditions report and using all caution when making the crossing to the Island. As a safer alternative to crossing the channel, you can cross at the ferry dock (see Trout Bay section on pg. 108 for directions) and then walk along the shore past the lighthouse to the climbs.

EAST CHANNEL

East Channel Curtains
✗ Kait Roszak
◯ Mike Wilkinson

East Channel Curtains ☐
WI3–5   10–40 meters

More of an experience than a route, these curtains extend along the entirety of the East Channel and never form the same way twice, making every experience a first experience.

Access to the top is often difficult making toproping a challenge, but for those willing to work for it, these curtains offers infinite possibilities and a lifetime of great climbing.

EAST CHANNEL

Between the *East Channel Curtains* and *I Get Your Point* there are several amazing sea caves that can offer a unique view and some interesting ice formations. You can't miss these caves as you make your way from the curtains toward Trout Point.

I Get Your Point ☐
WI3   25 meters
N46.4917 W86.6095

Not everyone sees it the same way but located in plain sight, a deep bowl sits south east of Trout Point. This remote sheet of ice is evocative of many of the East Channel climbs, being steep and sustained. Spend the day climbing these pumpy routes and your arms just might say, "I Get Your Point!"

Cave North of the
East Channel Curtains
Rachel Pohl
Max Lowe

TROUT BAY

TROUT BAY 20+ ROUTES • WI2–6 • 30–80m

Trout Bay is one of Munising's hidden gems. It can't be seen from anywhere on the mainland so it has eluded many climbers' attentions, but the local fisherman have known of its riches for years! Trout Bay has two sides, east and west. The east holds a plethora of climbs, all individually named and recognized, whereas the west side of Trout Bay is like the East Channel Curtains. It has "one" named route, but there is a season's worth of climbing opportunities on this 50-meter-high wall.

Getting into Trout Bay is easy, but impossible before the lake freezes. The best way is to leave from the Grand Island ferry dock and ski into Murray Bay. It is just over two miles to the isthmus that separates Murray from Trout Bay. Pick up the snowmobile trail on the isthmus and travel overland to the summertime cabins and sand beach of Trout Bay. From here, pick your destination and travel across the frozen bay to it.

Three Stooges
Mike Wilkinson

THE RAMPS

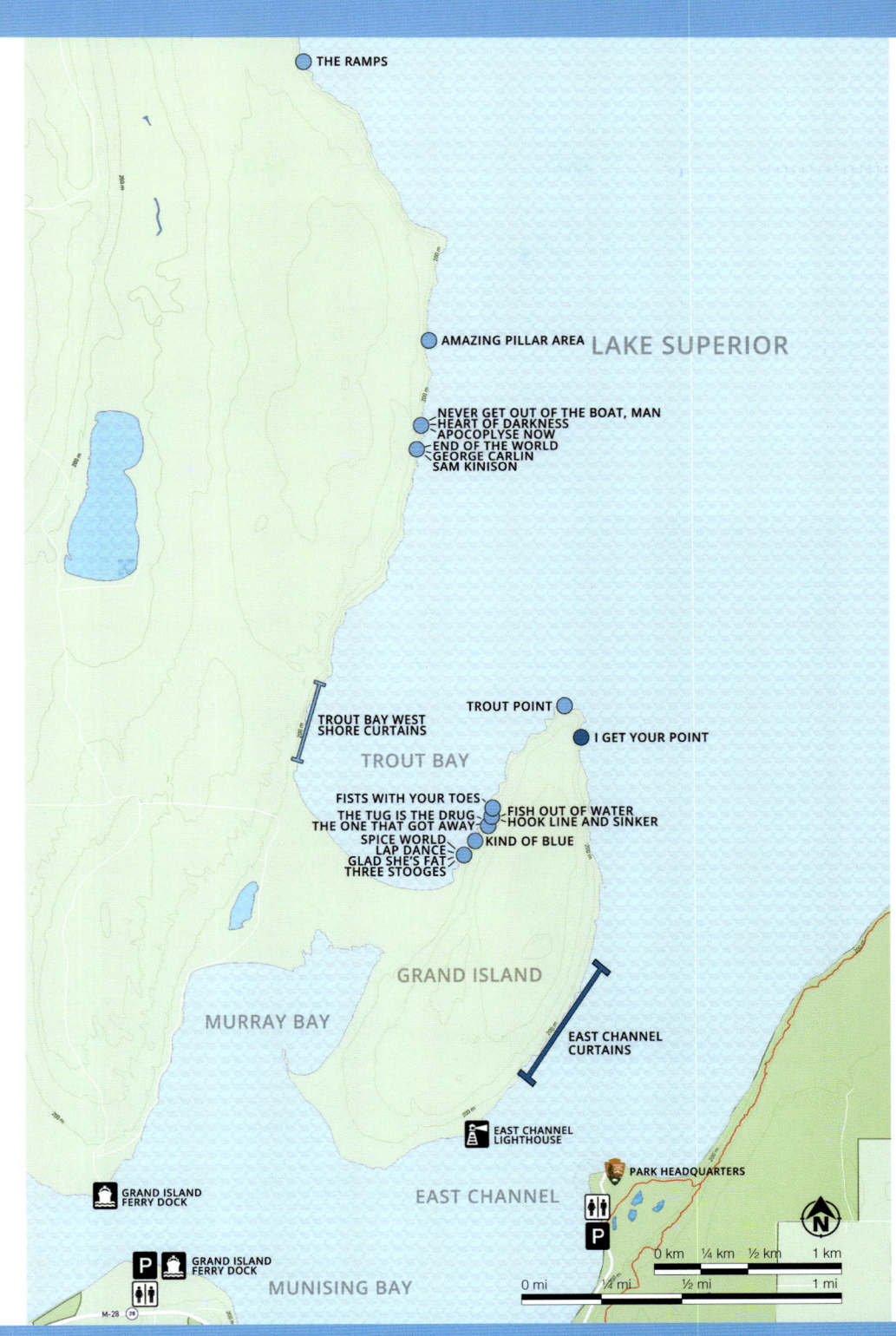

AMAZING PILLAR AREA

LAKE SUPERIOR

NEVER GET OUT OF THE BOAT, MAN
HEART OF DARKNESS
APOCOLYSE NOW
END OF THE WORLD
GEORGE CARLIN
SAM KINISON

TROUT POINT

TROUT BAY WEST
SHORE CURTAINS

I GET YOUR POINT

TROUT BAY

FISTS WITH YOUR TOES
THE TUG IS THE DRUG   FISH OUT OF WATER
THE ONE THAT GOT AWAY   HOOK LINE AND SINKER
SPICE WORLD
LAP DANCE   KIND OF BLUE
GLAD SHE'S FAT
THREE STOOGES

GRAND ISLAND

MURRAY BAY

EAST CHANNEL
CURTAINS

EAST CHANNEL
LIGHTHOUSE

PARK HEADQUARTERS

EAST CHANNEL

GRAND ISLAND
FERRY DOCK

GRAND ISLAND
FERRY DOCK

MUNISING BAY

0 km   ¼ km   ½ km   1 km
0 mi   ¼ mi   ½ mi   1 mi

TROUT BAY

Three Stooges ☐
WI3　　　　　11 meters　　　　　N46.4806 W86.6253

A fun, short pillar that is the first interesting piece of ice you will see. Usually quite small at the base, it gets bigger the higher you climb.

Glad She's Fat ☐
WI3　　　　12 meters
N46.4806 W86.6249

Another pillar of ice that sometimes grows into a curtain of ice. Just past *Three Stooges* this little climb is also worth getting on.

Three Stooges
📷 Mike Wilkinson

Lap Dance ☐
WI3　　　　　10 meters
N46.4807 W86.6245

The smallest of the first three formations, this climb will give you your money's worth.

Spice World ☐
WI2–3+　　　　10 meters
N446.4809 W86.6243

Spice World holds five climbs on a good year; *Scary*, *Sporty*, *Ginger* (the yellowest of the curtains in the middle) *Posh* and *Baby Spice*. They range from WI2 to WI3, and all are around 8 to 10 meters tall. They form differently year from year, but something will always be in and you will 'Wannabe' climbing it!

Glad She's Fat
✗ Unknown
📷 Matt Abbotts

Kind of Blue ☐
WI2–3　　　7–10 meters　　　　　N46.4819 W86.6230

Just past British girl power pop we enter the refined, slowed down world of jazz. Depending on seasonal conditions, another five climbs are located in this zone; *So What*, *Freddie Freeloader*, *Blue in Green*, *All Blues* and *Flamenco Sketches*. These climbs are all short, but fun nonetheless and offer a good warm up for the climbs found further down in *The Bowl*.

The Bowl holds the best climbing on the east side of Trout Bay. On a good year, five lines form offering both challenging and stimulating climbing just a short distance from the beach.

Fish Out of Water
X Jon Jugenheimer
📷 Erik Olsen

Fists With Your Toes ☐
WI3+   18 meters   N46.4848 W86.6209

A series of cascading steps from the cedar trees to the lake on the far left of *The Bowl*. This climb can be wide with multiple options and is a great place to prctice their leading skills.

The One That Got Away ☐
WI4   16 meters   N46.4836 W86.6218

The furthest right route in the bowl, this short, fun vertical curtain sometimes offers a finish to the left into the trees, otherwise rappel back to the ground on a V thread.

The Tug is the Drug ☐
WI4   17 meters   N46.4837 W86.6214

This climb doesn't always top out into the trees and ends on an almost vertical cliff with bad rock. It may be possible to lead out to the right and finish on a tree, otherwise best to rap back to the ground with a V thread.

Hook Line and Sinker ☐
WI4   17 meters   N46.4839 W86.6210

This is the easier of the four vertical climbs in *The Bowl*, and offers the best access to get to a tree anchor above. Stem between vertical columns and work up to the top of the flow.

Fish Out of Water ☐
WI5   18 meters   N46.4842 W86.6206

One of the more aesthetic lines in The Bowl, *Fish out of Water* climbs a vertical curtain to an overhanging buldge before a ramp into the trees. On your arms the whole way, you will be struggling to catch your breath while flailing your tools over the roof.

Hook Line and Sinker
X David Hixenbaugh
📷 Erik Olsen

Trout Point ☐
WI3   10 meters   N46.4848 W86.6200

Just south of Trout Point, which is located at the far northern point of the East Channel, several sheets of ice form consistently each year.

TROUT BAY

The west side of Trout Bay holds one of the best kept secrets in the entire region. The climbs are long, steep, demanding, and offer plenty of possibilities for intermediate and advanced climbers There are no distinct names for the west side of Trout Bay and you should experience it by walking up to the wall, picking a line and climbing it, creating a first experience all your own.

Ranging from WI3 to WI6, 10 to 55 meters, the walls are almost completely covered in ice on a good year and barely covered in a bad year. Routes will be almost impossible to find from above on the snowmobile trail, so wait for good lake ice conditions when you can ski directly to the base.

On sunny days during the early and late season it is critical to stay off the sun baked, thin ice, and south-facing climbs. The sandstone walls are perfect solar collectors, and whole sheets of ice have been known to collapse without warning.

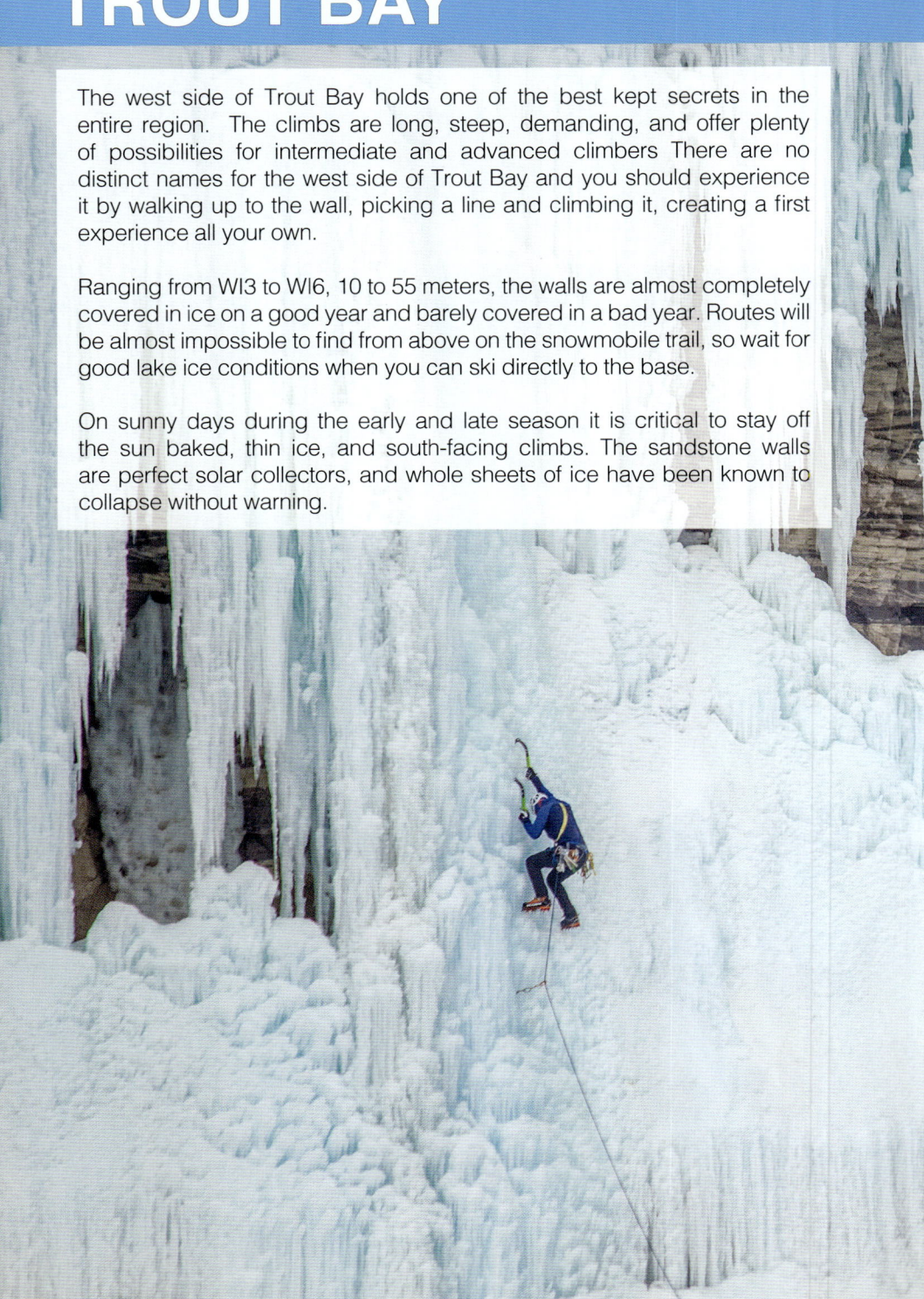

Trout Bay West Shore Curtains □
WI3–6   10–55 meters   N46.4937 W86.6446

The west side of Trout Bay is must-stop on the island tour. Half a mile wide and 55 meters tall at its highest point, the ice here is like a mini-Canadian Rockies. From vertical, challenging ice found in the middle of the formations, to the easy, lower angle rambling ice far on the left margin, there is something here for almost any climber capable of leading. White pillars of ice surrounded by slabs of yellow, gray and blue ice is the typical scenery found here. Expect to find multiple, separate lines in this zone, with the conditions changing throughout the season to make for a different experience every time you come back.

West Side of Trout Bay
David Hixenbaugh ✗
Jacob Raab 📷

TROUT BAY

To get to the six named climbs below, one must walk or ski north past the *Trout Bay West Shore Curtains*, then the climbs will start coming into view. The easiest way is to walk on the frozen lake; traveling on the snowmobile path above the lake will make the climbs very hard to find without a GPS. Once you get out of Trout Bay, and are exposed to the open waters of Lake Superior, the ice pack becomes thinner, and forms only in the coldest winters. Please exercise extreme caution while traveling on the lake ice in this area as conditions can change week to week or hour by hour depending on the wind. There are a dozen or so short, unnamed climbs between *Sam Kinison* and The West Side of Trout Bay that form on any regular year. They do not hold much interest to climb if you are journeying this far out.

End of the World
Jon Jugenheimer X
Erik Olsen

Sam Kinison ☐
WI4   40 meters
N46.5162 W86.6304

This is the first formation that you see when venturing past the West Side Ice. *Sam Kinison* is a close neighbor of *George Carlin*, and in fat years they could be considered the same climb. Climb the slab to the headwall, picking your line depending on the current conditions.

George Carlin ☐
WI4   45 meters
N46.5165 W86.6303

GC is the better, funnier line in this formation, located on the right margin of the flow. There is an independent pillar above the slab start. You will really understand yourself, and the world around you by climbing this line without using the seven dirty words along the way to get there.

End Of the World ☐
WI4   45 meters
N46.5166 W86.6303

This pillar is third line in this zone and is one of the best lines on the west side of Trout Bay. Start down and right of the pillar and climb the vertical headwall and ramp above. Then follow the pillar until you reach the small water source in the overhanging rock.

West Side of Trout Bay
David Hixenbaugh ✗
Emily Oppliger 📷

Apocalypse Now ☐
WI4+   45 meters
N46.5184 W86.6297

Apocalypse Now is found around a small buttress covered in cedar trees. Climb the vertical pillar of ice above the ramp, sometimes thin, sometimes fat, or sometimes not at all. Only then will you uncover, what you are looking for.

Heart of Darkness ☐
WI5   40 meters
N46.5185 W86.6297

The hardest climb in this group, this curtain offers the most sustained climbing. Start from the water by climbing a shallow ramp to a vertical free hanging curtain. In early season, it is nothing more than daggers.

Never Get Out of the Boat, Man. ☐
WI3+   45 meters   N46.5185 W86.6296

The easiest route in the area, offering a ramp of ice to a short, off vertical step into the trees above. This route can be identified easily as it's climber's left of a large rock buttress and a large birch tree leans out over the climb.

TROUT BAY

Amazing Pillar Area
WI5–6 30–55 meters
N46.5260 W86.6289

The *Amazing Pillar* is just one area past the named climbs at the end of Trout Bay that we are going to tell you about, the rest is left up to you for an adventure. If you choose to spend the time and energy to make it this far out, you will be rewarded with climbs that have never been touched by the cold steel of an ice pick, or at least not for many years as this is the area that sees the fewest climbers. The crown jewel of ice in this zone is formed off an overhanging cliff that pours ice over the lip to form many incredible, free standing pillars. The only issue is that there are way more than just one!

Amazing Pillar Area
Keith Ladzinski

The Ramps
WI4–6 50 meters
N46.4755 W86.5698

The Ramps is the other massive area on this side of the island that we are outlining. Mostly impossible to find from above without the use of GPS, and for sure almost impossible to scout conditions from above, *The Ramps* offer incredible climbing for only the most adventurous climber. Start from the lake by climbing long, low angling ramps of ice and snow to set a belay. Finish the line of your choosing by climbing the vertical headwall above for anywhere from 10 to 30 meters and into the trees.

WEST SHORE

West Side Curtains
Jon Jugenheimer ✗
Mike Wilkinson 📷

WEST SHORE   40+ ROUTES • WI2–6 • 30–80m

The West Shore of Grand Island should be on your tick list. It's wild, it's removed and it's an ice climbing experience you can't find anywhere else in the world. The best time to make the journey here is from late February well into March when the lake is frozen solid and packed with snow, when all of the routes are in and the sun is high in the sky providing the warmth needed to combat the winds blowing across the lake from Canada. The West Shore is what we wait for the other 10 months of the year when climbing here isn't possible, it is the most sought-after real estate on the island, but once there you will rarely see another person.

The best approach, other than the 30 minutes it would take on a snowmobile, is to ski from the Grand Island ferry dock and head straight for the southwest tip of the island which is about a mile and a half away. Once you round the corner, its only another mile to the first group of climbs: Spiral Staircase to Air Boat Dave. From the first zone, it is another 2 mile ski to Cedar Creek Falls. From Cedar Creek it's another 2.5 miles to the Northwest tip of the island, which starts the North Shore section of this book. The ski is totally flat, and once the pack ice fills in with windblown snow, you will be at the climbs in no time!

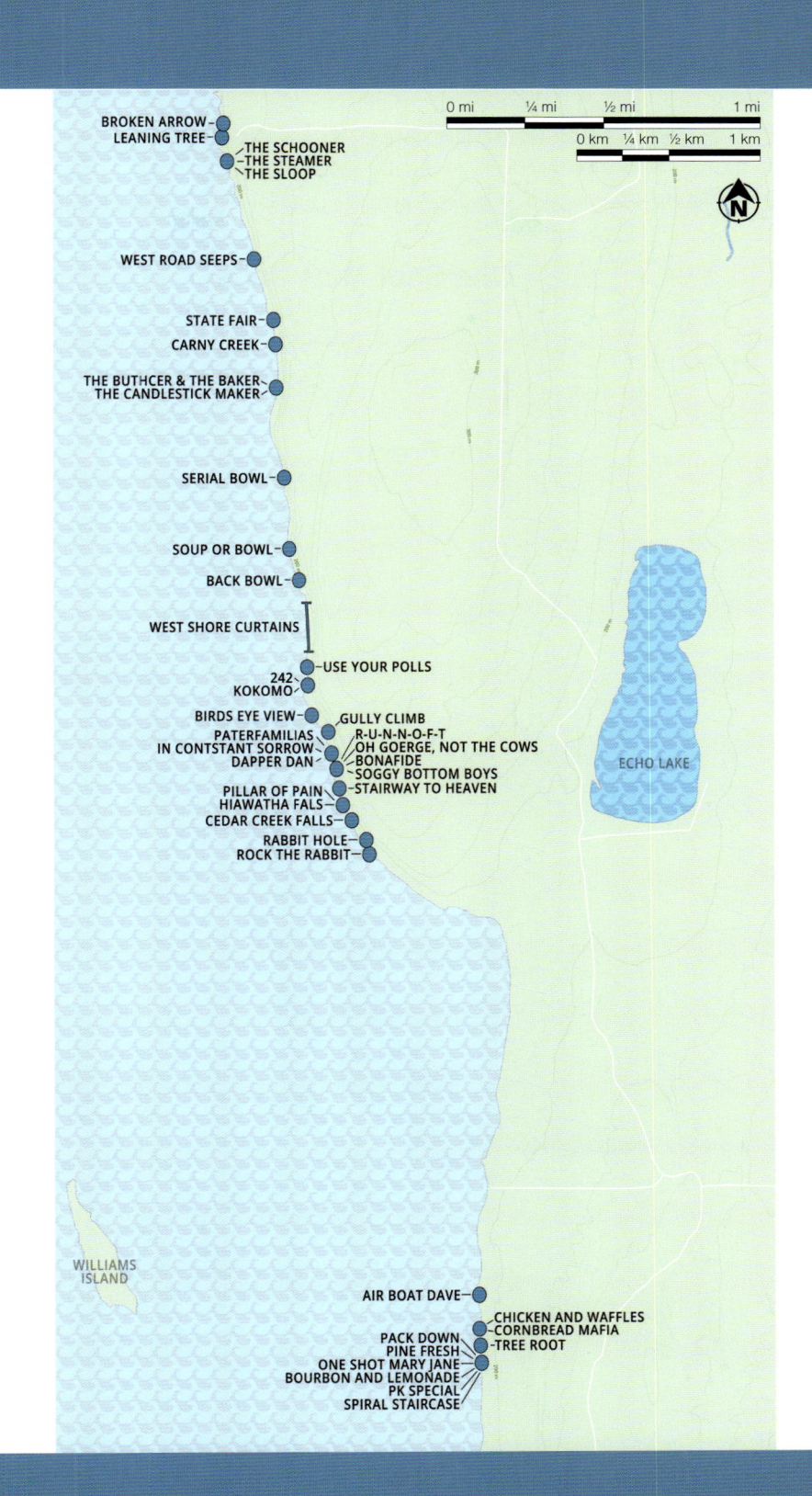

BROKEN ARROW
LEANING TREE
THE SCHOONER
THE STEAMER
THE SLOOP

WEST ROAD SEEPS

STATE FAIR
CARNY CREEK

THE BUTHCER & THE BAKER
THE CANDLESTICK MAKER

SERIAL BOWL

SOUP OR BOWL
BACK BOWL

WEST SHORE CURTAINS

USE YOUR POLLS
242
KOKOMO
BIRDS EYE VIEW
GULLY CLIMB
PATERFAMILIAS
R-U-N-N-O-F-T
IN CONTSTANT SORROW
OH GOERGE, NOT THE COWS
DAPPER DAN
BONAFIDE
SOGGY BOTTOM BOYS
PILLAR OF PAIN
STAIRWAY TO HEAVEN
HIAWATHA FALS
CEDAR CREEK FALLS
RABBIT HOLE
ROCK THE RABBIT

ECHO LAKE

WILLIAMS ISLAND

AIR BOAT DAVE
CHICKEN AND WAFFLES
CORNBREAD MAFIA
PACK DOWN
TREE ROOT
PINE FRESH
ONE SHOT MARY JANE
BOURBON AND LEMONADE
PK SPECIAL
SPIRAL STAIRCASE

111

WEST SHORE

Spiral Staircase ☐
WI5   15 meters
N46.4756 W86.6861

Steep, technical ice leads to a ramp into the trees. "Twisting" ice requires careful thought.

PK Special ☐
WI4+   18 meters
N46.4756 W86.6861

Climb the ramp of ice to a freestanding pillar. Check the connection point on the overhanging rock before ascending, as this climb is known to fracture.

Bourbon and Lemonade ☐
WI3   20 meters   N46.4757 W86.6861

Ramping WI2–3 leads to a mellow top out, or take the right most line for more vertical ice.

One Shot Mary Jane ☐
WI3   20 meters   N46.4758 W86.6861

Ascend the ramp to a short vertical section. Climb through the ice bulges to the top.

Pine Fresh ☐
WI4   22 meters   N46.4760 W86.6861

This climb and its neighbors *Pack Down* and *Tree Root* have the most sustained vertical sections of climbing on this wall. Steep, dirty ramp leads to a vertical column.

PK Special
✘ : Jon Jugenheimer
📷 : Joe Stylos

Pack Down ☐
WI4   18 meters   N46.4762 W86.6861

Climb the steep ramp of ice, to a steeper column of ice above into the trees.

Tree Root
Heath Rowland : ✗
Mike Wilkinson : 📷

Tree Root ☐
WI4   20 meters
N46.4768 W86.6864

A noticeably blue column climbs steep ice to a bulge for a rest before making an airy traverse left. Two more moves up and grab onto any solid tree roots to get the send. Fun!

Cornbread Mafia ☐
WI3   20 meters
N46.4775 W86.6863

Most prominent line along a wide section of ice. Snow and ice ramp leads to wet ice for a short ride to the top.

Chicken and Waffles ☐
WI3   13 meters   N 46.4776 W86.6863

Delicious! Climb the short line, furthest left ice in this zone, licking your fingers the whole way.

WEST SHORE

Air Boat Dave
WI3–4 18 meters N46.4797 W86.6863

Air Boat Dave is a five-minute walk past *Chicken & Waffles* and is located where the cliff ramps back up, before diving again into the beaches that make up Mather Bay. Air Boat is a series of curtains and pillars that flow directly from the ground water seeping out of the cliff band. Most lines do not go all the way to the top of the cliff.

Cedar Creek Falls
Erik Olsen
Jon Jugenheimer

Rock the Rabbit
WI4 35 meters
N46.5033 W86.6959

This is the first climb located up the West Shore past Mather Bay and not far from the historic Play Boy Club located on the Island. On the right side of the first large rock buttress this large, bulbous climb starts as a ramp from lake level, then turns vertical before you reach the cedar trees above.

Rabbit Hole
WI3 35 meters
N46.5037 W86.6963

This hole is found left of the rock buttress noted above, providing multiple climbing options depending on conditions. Climb up the right ramp with a short vertical step one third of the way up, or climb the left side with more sustained vertical ice, with good rests on the micro ledges found on the route.

Cedar Creek Falls ☐
WI3   17 meters   N46.5050 W86.6975

Ceder Creek is listed on all USGS maps, and is an easy identifier to locate where you are. This short waterfall freezes up as a cone of ice and is usually hollow in the middle. The falls form directly onto the shelf ice in a small amphitheater surrounding the cone. Above the cone, the creek flows for another 60+ meters above into the woods, but the juice isn't worth the squeeze.

Cornbread Mafia
Heath Rowland ✗
Mike Wilkinson 📷

Hiawatha Falls ☐
WI5   50 meters   N46.5056 W86.6981

This two-tiered climb is reminiscent of the ice found in Cody, WY, but rather located in the flat world of the Midwest. Climb the vertical curtain or pillar to the ledge above. Fire the second vertical step to the top of this rope stretching pitch.

Pillar of Pain ☐
WI4   25 meters   N46.5065 W86.6988

The *Pillar of Pain* is more of a curtain than a pillar on any given year, but no matter how it forms, your forearms will be throbbing. Most people stop at the top of the vertical pitch. You can continue up the drainage if you choose but you'd better bring a machete rather than your ice tools.

Stairway to Heaven ☐
WI4   50 meters   N46.5065 W86.6988

This long, multi-tiered climb is a Midwest replica of the San Juan classic of the same name. Starting at the lake level, climb three vertical steps with good rests found between each one. Descend with two ropes from the trees above.

Approaching the West Side Climbs
Matt Abbotts 📷

WEST SHORE

O Brother Where Art Thou Wall

This large prominent bowl is one of the many gems that make up the spectacular West Shore of Grand Island. Easily recognizable as the bowl is separated in the middle by a line of cedar trees. A great way to soak up the sun and spend the afternoon picking off some bonafide routes.

Dapper Dan
X Linda Wappner
📷 Matt Abbotts

Soggy Bottom Boys ☐
WI3   50 meters
N46.5079 W86.6988

Tucked in the righthand side corner of the furthest right curtain, this rampy shaded 50 meter climb is super enjoyable… unless you start this pitch off with the dreaded soggy bottoms. Beware of thin ice in the late spring!

BonaFide ☐
WI4   70 meters
N46.508093 W86.698918

This proud line is the obvious yellowish color center line of the right hand curtain. Follow the ramp to where ice daggers overhang the rock wall, carefully work your way onto the vertical ice and then to the exit ramps above. Top out and tell 'em "I'm Bonafide, what are you?"

Oh George, Not the Cows ☐
WI3   45 meters
N46.5076 W86.6988

Located on the right curtains, this climb starts with a low-angle ramp, often covered in snow to the steep vertical blue columns of ice. Bring in your second off of the solid conifer trees at the top.

R-U-N-N-O-F-T ☐
WI3   60 meters
N46.5082 W86.6990

If Mrs. Hogwallop up and R-U-N-N-O-F-T she would do it up the far left hand side of the right hand curtain.

Oh Brother Where Art Thou Wall
Jake Bourdow 📷

Soggy Bottom Boys
Matt Abbotts ✗
Bill Thompson 📷

Gearing up below the right curtain
Bill Thompson 📷

Dapper Dan ☐
WI3   65 meters
N46.5085 W86.6990

"Well, I don't want Fop, goddamn it! I'm a Dapper Dan man!"

If you want our *Dapper Dan*, climb the right hand side of the left curtain. Ascend just to the left of the tree line. Climb up to the small cedar trees halfway up then move left toward the center of the curtains to some bushes/roots for anchors. Can be done as two pitches. Take note that this route stays out of the spring sun.

In Constant Sorrow ☐
WI4   60 meters
N46.5087 W86.6992

Pick a line in the center of this curtain which often has streams of ice interspersed with rocky sections. This section can be susceptible to the intense heat of the sun during the late spring.

Paterfamilias ☐
WI3   50 meters
N86.6993 W46.5089

"I'll tell you what I am, I'm the damn paterfamilias"

... and so is the far left climb of the left curtain. Similar to the other climbs on this curtain, start off on a rampy section that progresses into a more vertical section.

WEST SHORE

Gully Climb
X Arni Ronis
📷 Matt Abbotts

Gully Climb
WI2 48 meters N46.5095 W86.6995

A rampy climb that offers easy to moderate climbing in a gully that reaches the rim of Grand Island. Climb under the fallen tree and up the ramps to gain the top of the climb. For those interested, a short slog through the snow leads to a short 4 meter vertical sheet of ice, enabling climbers to get a "second" pitch in.

Bird's Eye View
Kendra Stritch X
Jake Bourdow 📷

Bird's Eye View
WI3 60 meters
N46.5107 W86.7009

A small bowl south of a large rock buttress, and north of the obvious *Gully Climb*. *Bird's Eye View* can form as three separate lines, or one large sheet of ice covering the top vertical step in the bowl. Climb a multi tiered ramp for the first 20 meters, then pick your vertical finish into the trees.

Kokomo
WI3   30 meters   N46.5121 W86.7012

Just past the large rock buttress, this low-angled climb is one of the easiest on the West Shore. Climb the snow and ice ramp into the steps above. The top of this route displays some wind sculpted ice that creates an interesting finish! It is fast climbing off the ice, but then you must take it slow once you figure out where you want to go.

242
WI3   30 meters
N46.5125 W86.7011

This climb is on the left side of a wide bowl of ice and offers a fantastic lead to get you warmed up for the *West Shore Curtains*. Climb the lower-angle ice, with some small vertical steps to keep it interesting.

Use Your Polls
WI3   40 meters
N46.5132 W86.7012

The last climb right before you get to the *West Shore Curtains* offers steep climbing, but much shorter than its more popular neighbor. Climb the low angle ice and snow ramp to the steep headwall above.

West Shore Curtains
Arni Ronis
Matt Abbotts

Paterfamilias
Arni Ronis
Matt Abbotts

WEST SHORE

West Shore Curtains
WI2–6 48 meters
N46.5159 W86.7011

This, this is why you are climbing on the Island. This amazing, homogeneous "mile of ice" can't be believed until you see for yourself and sink your tools and front points into it. Cascading directly to the lakeshore, climb the snow-covered ice for 10–20 meters until you can dig your way out of the depths of the accumulated lake effect snow and onto the steeper ice. Climb the line of your choosing, vertical ice pillars with umbrella structures in the middle, or ramping ice on the periphery. The *West Shore Curtains* are a good destination for all experience levels in your party.

West Shore Curtains
X Jon Jugenheimer
📷 Mike Wilkinson

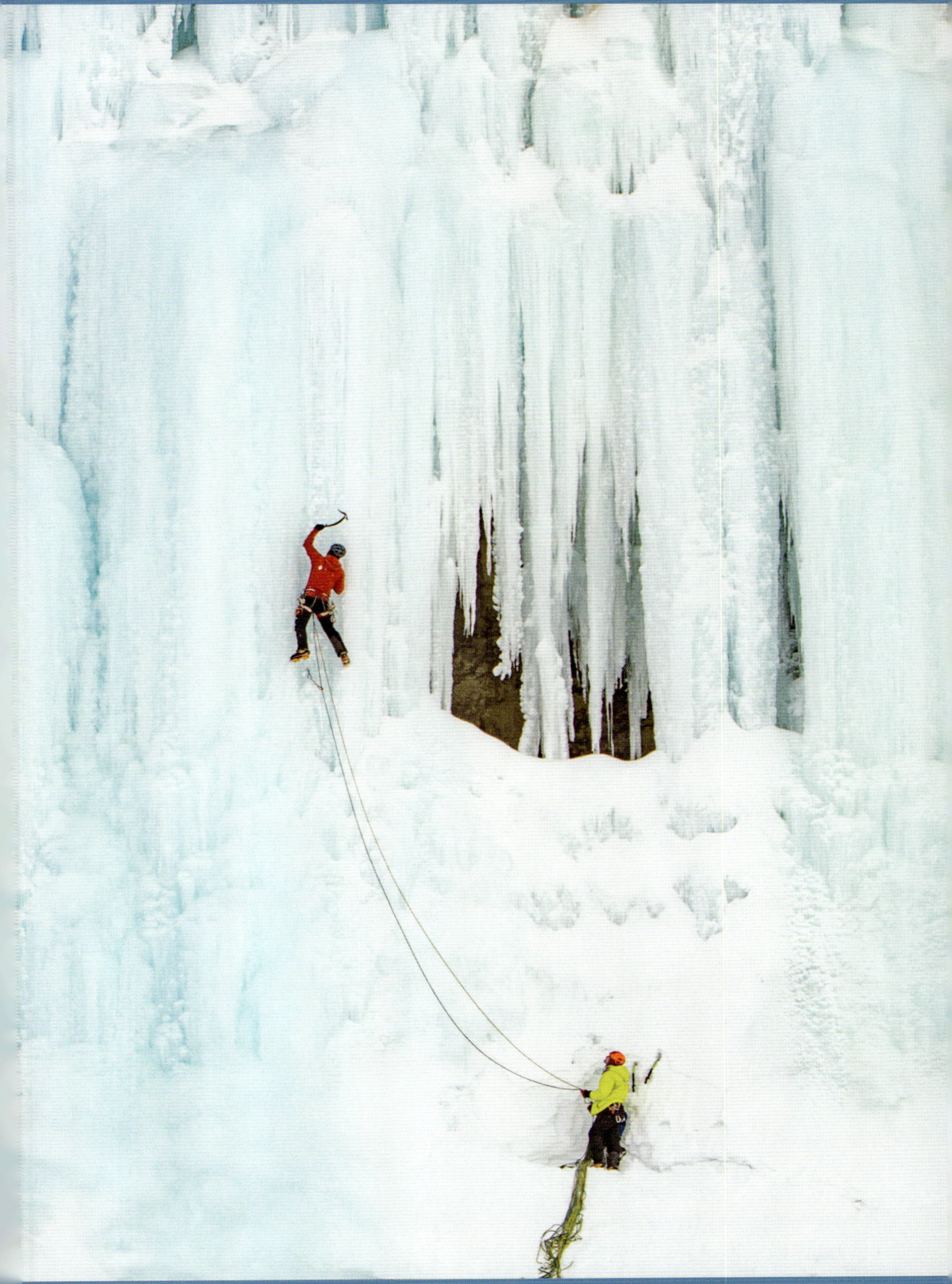

WEST SHORE

Back Bowl
WI3　　　　　　　　　45 meters
N46.5180 W86.7018

Past the next rock buttress, you'll find the *Back Bowl* of the *West Shore Curtains*. Climb the snow slope into a bowl hosting a steep wall of ice, with snow and ice ramps and vertical steps above.

Soup or Bowl
WI3+　　45 meters　　N46.5197 W86.7028

Located one rock buttress past *Back Bowl*, this climb is much wider than the previous, and a bit harder. Like the other two bowls, this climb is vertical steps mixed with snowy ramps, but steeper, longer verticals prove it truly is a super bowl.

Serial Bowl
WI3　　　　　　45 meters　　　　　　N46.5236 W86.7031

The last of the Bowl climbs, this is the easiest of the three, and a further walk from the *West Shore Curtains* than the first two combined. Motor on past *Soup or Bowl* for 5–10 minutes of walking or skiing, to find this large, slightly southwest-facing bowl of ice. More of a cascade flow of low-angle ice with very short vertical steps this route is a great place for a first time lead.

West Shore Curtains
Adam Dailey
Mike Wilkinson

Candlestick Maker
WI5   35 meters
N46.5283 W86.7040

This is an amazing freestanding pillar of ice and one of the "must do" climbs on the West Shore of Grand Island. Start up the short headwall of ice that makes up the base of the pillar, inspect the structural integrity of what you are about to climb then fire! Climb the path of least resistance for 20+ meters while on your arms the whole way. Once on top of the pillar, tread lightly over the attachment point. Follow the short remaining steps of ice above to a large birch tree.

The Butcher & The Baker
WI4   40 meters
N46.5289 W86.7039

This is the large ice sheet climber's left of the *Candle Stick Maker*. Climb the two vertical steps separated by a large snow ledge at half height. Multiple climbable options can be found on this piece of ice and it forms regularly, where as its neighbor may come and go through the same season.

WEST SHORE

Carny Creek ☐
WI3 45 meters
N46.5308 W86.7040

This long, narrow climb is an unnamed creek found on most topo maps and usually is quite wet through most of the season. Begin by climbing the long, low angle ice and snow ramp into the trees about half way up the cliff face. Climb the vertical step above that leads to the top of the cliffline and into the trees.

State Fair ☐
WI3–4 40 meters
N46.5320 W86.7043

The next large, obvious climb is another "must do" on the west side of the Island. Climb up intermittent steps of vertical ice separated by snow, picking your line of least, or maximum, resistance as you go.

Gearing up for a climb on the West Shore
Adam Dailey & Jon Jugenheimer
Mike Wilkinson

West Road Seeps ☐
WI2–4 30–40 meters N46.5355 W86.7061

The seeps in this zone are a collection of climbs, rather than one individual climb. Between *State Fair* and *The Sloop*, over a dozen independent lines can form (or not) all ranging from WI2 to WI4 with none of them being remarkable or eye catching in any way. Most people travel past them to other climbs, but note that they exist, and can still provide a good fallback option to or from a better climb.

The Sloop, The Steamer, and the Schooner ☐
WI3- 25 meters N46.5404 W86.7082

Nearing the northwest point of the island, but not quite there yet, and hidden from view if traveling on the lakeshore, are these three almost identical climbs. Just past a geologically interesting prow of rock (check it out, you won't be disappointed) three independent slabs of ice are found. Climb the slab for 15–25 meters to a short vertical section of ice to the trees above. Note, sometimes these climbs do not form all the way to the top of the cliff.

Candlestick Maker
Jon Jugenheimer
Erik Olsen

Leaning Tree
WI2 25 meters
N46.5421 W86.7087

Almost to the northwest tip of the island, *Leaning Tree* is a small flow similar in nature to the ship climbs above, but not as steep.

Broken Arrow
WI3 25 meters
N46.5426 W86.7087

The twin brother to *Leaning Tree*, the climb is only meters to the left of it and tops out in the same location.

NORTH SHORE

NORTH SHORE   **20 ROUTES • WI3–5 • 20–70m**

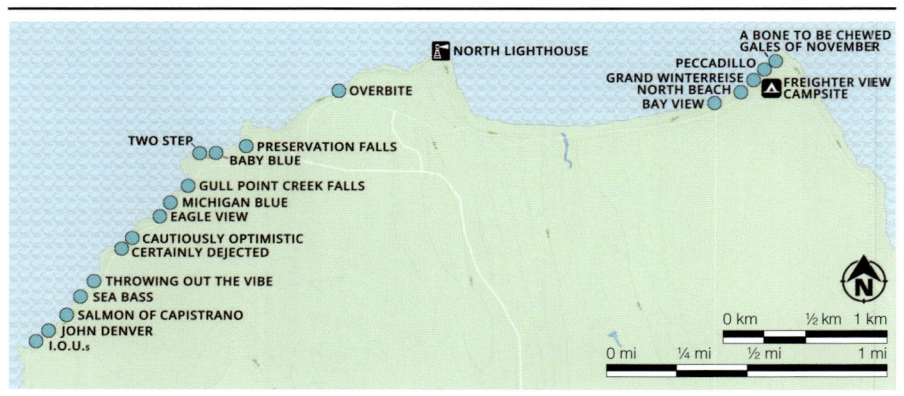

Map locations:
- NORTH LIGHTHOUSE
- A BONE TO BE CHEWED
- GALES OF NOVEMBER
- PECCADILLO
- GRAND WINTERREISE
- NORTH BEACH
- BAY VIEW
- FREIGHTER VIEW CAMPSITE
- OVERBITE
- TWO STEP
- PRESERVATION FALLS
- BABY BLUE
- GULL POINT CREEK FALLS
- MICHIGAN BLUE
- EAGLE VIEW
- CAUTIOUSLY OPTIMISTIC
- CERTAINLY DEJECTED
- THROWING OUT THE VIBE
- SEA BASS
- SALMON OF CAPISTRANO
- JOHN DENVER
- I.O.U.s

Michigan Blue
X Angela VanWiemeersch
📷 Scott Crady

Commitment:
"The state or quality of being dedicated to a cause, or activity."

Exploring the North Shore of Grand Island takes a dedicated and hardy individual, as these climbs are by far the most difficult to access in the Upper Peninsula. The commitment is well rewarded, and these are some of the best routes (and least climbed!) in the area. The fruit of your hard work is sometimes the sweetest!

Besides being a challenge to get to, the North Shore is vulnerable to the brutal north winds blowing across Lake Superior from Canada, which turns the area into a vast windswept tundra. This ain't Colorado, so climbing in belay parkas is not unheard of. The payoff is that the views from the top of the pitches are spectacular panoramas of a landscape that resembles the Arctic more than it does Michigan.

To the truly devoted, human-powered travel will take a full day to access the climbs via the inner trail system on the island. For those with a sled, take the same trails and cut the approach time down but still plan on several hours to access the climbs.

Two Step
Raphael Slawinski
Mike Wilkinson

NORTH SHORE

IOUs ☐
WI3　　　　　　　　　　25 meters
N46.5452 W86.7080

John Denver ☐
WI3　　　　　　　　　　25 meters
N46.5458 W86.7071

Salmon of Capistrano ☐
WI3　　　　　　　　　　25 meters
N46.5467 W86.7058

Sea Bass ☐
WI3　　　　　　　　　　25 meters
N46.54766 W86.70478

Throwing out the Vibe ☐
WI3　　25 meters　　　　N46.5484 W86.7038

These five climbs are very similar in nature, and all found in the same stretch of cliff. They are located from just north of the northwest tip of the island where the snowmobile path intersection is, to the prow of rock just south of *Certainly Dejected*. All five are just off-vertical starting as steep ramps from the lake, to vertical finishes into the trees. The ice thickness will vary from season to season and route to route, but this general zone holds five great climbs to tick off your list on any given winter.

Looking west at IOUs, John Denver, etc.
📷 Jon Jugenheimer

Certainly Dejected ☐
WI4　　　　　　　　　　30 meters
N46.5502 W86.7018

This climb forms very similarly to *Cautiously Optimistic*, as it is located just right of it in the same small bowl. Climb the steep ramp of ice to the vertical finish, watch for the sting in the tail.

Cautiously Optimistic ☐
WI4　　　　　　　　　　30 meters
N46.5506 W86.7011

A thin ramp of ice, sometimes only taking stubbies over half way up finishing on windblown, three-dimensional ice above. One must be a true optimist to finish the line in the conditions found during the first ascent.

Eagle View ☐
WI4　　23 meters　　　　N46.5518 W86.6990

Eagle View is climber's right of *Michigan Blue*, and isn't always visible from above. Hidden below an overhanging rock roof, this climb forms differently each season, sometimes forming to the top of the cliff, sometimes not. Sometimes it is an easy vertical curtain of ice, sometimes it is a horror show of ice and daggers above your head to make you run away.

Michigan Blue ☐
WI4   25 meters   N46.5525 W86.6982

Being the most aesthetic climb on the North Shore with an unsurpassed view, this climb is one not to miss while climbing way out here on this side of the island. A series of daggers and fangs weld together by early January to make a large curtain of ice, ranging from deep blue to white in color. Many options are usualy availabe to pick from to lead back out from the lake below.

Michigan Blue
✕ Jon Jugenheimer
📷 Aaron Peterson

Gull Point Creek Falls ☐
WI3-4   20 meters
N46.5534 W86.6969

This waterfall is easy to find as there is a concrete bridge over the creek above. It starts as a yellow ramp to a ledge halfway up where it gets steeper, with overhanging rock on both sides.

Two Step ☐
WI4   12 meters
N46.5550 W86.6959

Although short, these two daggers are pumpy! Climb one of the touching daggers, while using the other to back step to the top. There is a small ice shelf below this climb to keep your feet dry while on belay.

Baby Blue ☐
WI2+   10 meters
N46.5550 W86.6948

This short, easy climb west of *Preservation Falls* can be identified by its striking blue color. It usually ends on a small shelf of boulders and beach making it climbable if the lake isn't frozen below.

Preservation Falls ☐
WI3   20 meters
N46.5554 W86.6926

The small falls at the mouth of Preservation Creek. The falls are usually wet, but consistently form each season.

Overbite ☐
WI5   40 meters   N46.5584 W86.6857

Located southwest of the lighthouse, this is the first climb you will encounter on the North Shore when approaching via the center road. At the final T intersection take a left, and *Overbite* will be located where the trail nears the lakeshore and turns to the southwest. This climb is steep and consists of up to 4 fangs that meld into a curtain later in the season.

NORTH SHORE

Freighter View Area
📷 Bill Thompson

Bay View ☐
WI4　　　20 meters
N46.5578 W86.6584

This climb is the closest regularly forming route to the beach. Climb the ramp to the steep headwall above.

Grand Winterreise ☐
WI4+　　　25 meters
N46.5594 W86.6549

This is the hardest route in the zone and doesn't always form each season. Climb the vertical curtain with the angle backing off the higher you get into the drainage above.

North Beach ☐
WI3+　　　20 meters
N46.5585 W86.6565

This off-vertical piece of ice is usually yellow, and has a snow bench one third of the way up providing a great rest before blasting to the top.

The six climbs between the the North Shore Lighthouse and the Freighter View campsite all come into condition on an average year, with the potential for more (or less) on any given year. All of these climbs are located between Freighter View on the North East point of the Island and the North Beach with the lighthouse further to the west. The easiest way to approach the climbs is to snowmobile up the center road of the Island then take a right (east) at the last T intersection and follow it past the beach to the climbs. A great way to scope conditions is to stop at Freighter View, look back to the west and you should be able to see most of the climbs from there.

Gales of November ☐
WI3   25 meters
N46.5597 W86.6542

This climb doesn't form all the way to the top of the cliff as it is fed by groundwater flowing through the rock strata. Climb the ramp to a short vertical step to finish the line. You may be able to get to the trees above to make an anchor; otherwise you will need to make a V thread to descend.

Peccadillo   ☐
WI3   25 meters
N46.5594 W86.6549

Don't offend your partner by claiming the lead on this short, moderate line found flowing from the cracks in the rocks. This climb also doesn't always form to the top of the cliff, buyer beware.

A Bone to Be ☐ Chewed
WI4   25 meters
N46.5598 W86.6540

Found closest to the Freighter View overlook, climb the thin verglass on a prominent wall just west of a small alcove. This route usually gets thicker further into the season.

There is nothing that gets us more stoked than something brand new. It can be something as simple as a new pair of socks or a new set of tools, but on the top of our list has to be a new ice climbing crag! The excitement of climbing in a new area adds to the "first experience" and restores the sense of discovery that is at the heart of our sport. The following sections of this book are dedicated to this sense of adventure and exploring new crags. And, as a bonus, if it is solitude that you seek, these ice crags can provide tranquil, challenging, virgin ice that one shares only with those willing to explore the backwoods and backroads of the Upper Peninsula.

Surveying the Landscape
Bill Thompson : X
Aaron Peterson : 📷

ROCK RIVER CANYON

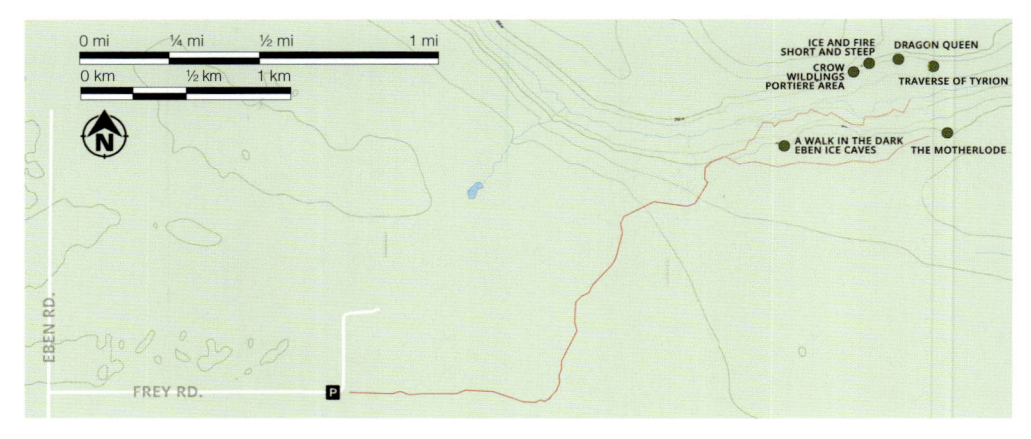

ROCK RIVER CANYON
10 ROUTES • WI2–4 • 5–9m

The Rock River Canyon Wilderness Area is located in Alger County southwest of Munising. Two rivers, Rock River and Silver Creek, flow through 150-foot-deep canyons which are separated by a broad flatland covered in hardwood forest. At the edges of the canyons are sandstone outcroppings much like the rock formations found in Munising. Wind and water have sculpted small caves along the ridges and in the winter they are filled with ice.

From M-94 in Eben Junction turn north onto Eben Road and drive about 1.5 miles to Frey Road. Turn right on Frey Road and drive to the end. Park along the road. There are often a lot of snowshoers, skiers and other visitors, so try to minimize your impact. The best times to climb at the actual Eben Ice Caves is very early mornings or after dark in the middle of the week.

Fire and Ice
X Linda Wappner
📷 Bill Thompson

Eben Ice Caves
David Hixenbaugh X
Bill Thompson

ROCK RIVER CANYON

Wildlings
X David Hixenbaugh
📷 Bill Thompson

Eben Ice Caves ☐
WI3   6 meters   N46.3828 W86.9445

Fed from a swamp above, the ice drops over the sandstone bluff in an ice curtain which encases the cave. This is a popular tourist destination making it impossible to climb on weekends. The 60-foot-wide curtain is short by any standards but can be fun to run laps on.

A Walk In The Dark ☐
WI2   5 meters   N46.3829 W86.9444

This short climb offers the beginner a little easier introduction to Michigan Ice. One of the easiest leads in Rock River Canyon.

The Motherlode
📷 Bill Thompson

The Motherlode ☐
WI3   9 meters
N46.3831 W86.9385

Located a short walk past *Eben Ice Caves*, this set of curtains develop into an overhanging, tiered formation with hanging daggers guarding the top. This 70 foot wide curtain offers several interesting lines.

Dragon Queen ☐
WI4   8 meters
N46.3851 W86.9403

Guarded by a large cedar tree above, this vertical formation is wider at the bottom and funnels to a narrow exit at the top near the tree.

Crow ☐
WI3   7 meters
N46.3849 W86.9415

A vertical to overhanging start leads to a more relaxed section at the top.

Traverse of Tyrion ☐
N46.3849 W86.9391

The climbs in this sandstone bowl only rise halfway up the cliff and not over the overhanging roof. While short in stature, link the seeps for an amazing pump on this long sustained traverse.

Ice and Fire ☐
WI3   9 meters   N46.3850 W86.9411

A lower vertical section eases off and mellows the closer you get to the top

Wildlings ☐
WI3   6 meters   N46.3848 W86.9419

This hanging curtain drops a few thin pillars. The right pillar is butted up against a large dead tree.

Spring on the Traverse of Tyrion
Bill Thompson ✗
Linda Wappner 📷

The Portière Area ☐
WI3   7 meters   N46.3846 W86.9418

Several very short lines are available in this long curtained area. As a warmup, run laps on a line or two.

The Subway ☐
WI3   9 meters   N46.3909 W87.0689

The Subway is the other classic in the Rock River Canyon outside of the Ice Caves. Climb a small, off-vertical flow, finding large pine trees above for anchors. A perfect place to find via a backcountry ski tour, as this climb is more of an adventure than a destination.

For easiest access take M-94 west of Munising 28 miles to Sundell, just west of Chatham. Turn right (north) on Dorsey Road in Sundell for about 2.5 miles. Park in the Laughing Whitefish Falls parking lot or where the plowing ends. Ski or snowshoe back in.

MARQUETTE COUNTY

Marquette, the largest city in the Upper Peninsula, is a major port on Lake Superior known primarily for the shipping of iron ore. Due in part to its natural setting, thriving arts scene, and proximity to an abundance of year-round outdoor recreational opportunities, it was voted *Best in Travel 2017* by *Lonely Planet*. Marquette offers all of the resources of any city, and has become the hub of the south shore of Lake Superior for both business and culture. So if you're looking for climbing with a bit of "big city" style, schedule some time to explore around Marquette, you won't be disappointed.

People rarelt think about Marquette and ice climbing as it is often overshadowed by the plethora of ice routes by its neighbor to the east. While we all love the classics in Munising, maybe you are looking for an area to have all to yourself? Climbing here has a sense of adventure as many of the routes are hidden in the backcountry and offer a peaceful wilderness setting. The fact that many of these places sit on the edge of the largest freshwater lake in the world doesn't hurt either!

Black Rocks Bouldering
Ross Herr X
Bill Thompson

BURNS LANDING
BIG BAY
LAKE SUPERIOR
SCRATCH WALL
RED ROAD
LITTLE PRESQUE
HOGBACK MOUNTAIN
PRESQUE ISLE
MARQUETTE

MARQUETTE COUNTY

Presque Isle
A city park in Marquette, Presque Isle is a 323-acre forested, oval-shaped peninsula that juts into Lake Superior. Primarily a place to go bouldering, the setting might make it worthy of a stop as the climbing is situated directly above the crashing waves of Lake Superior.

Directions
From downtown Marquette, follow the scenic Lake Shore Boulevard north for about three miles and you will find yourself at the park's entrance. The road around the island is closed in the winter so the fastest way to access Black Rocks is to park at the Presque Isle Pavilion and walk clockwise around the island.

Black Rocks Bouldering ☐
N46.5901 W87.3770

Lots of high ball, low angle rocks that rise out of Lake Superior. Spend the morning running laps and enjoying a beautiful sunrise!

Turf War ☐
WI4 14 meters
N46.5805 W87.3802

This seldom-formed small drip is located inside a cave that can only be accessed from the lake ice when Lake Superior freezes. It is a challenging, slightly overhanging pillar. Please note the rock surrounding this climb is extremely unstable!

Black Rocks Bouldering
X Ross Herr
📷 Bill Thompson

140

Little Presque

Located just north of Marquette, this unique area is a short walk across lake ice to a small island covered in ice by the repeated blasts of Lake Superior's waves. The northern most part of the island offers endless bouldering and a few highball problems. During colder years, lake ice piles up along the sand beach on the mainland reaching heights of 25 feet and offers the opportunity to boulder on "glacier" type ice!

Directions

From downtown Marquette, follow the scenic Lake Shore Boulevard north. At the intersection with Haley Street turn left (Haley Street will turn into CR550). Drive 7.5 miles until you see the Michigan DNR sign on the right hand side of the road. Depending on the road condition you may have to park on CR550 and walk back to the island. If the road is drivable, drive back to the parking lot and make the short hike back to Lake Superior and the Island. **SAFETY NOTE:** You can only access the island if there is a stable ice bridge. Please check the local conditions report or call Down Wind Sports to get the beta.

Lakeshore Climb ☐
WI4 10 meters
N46.6242 W87.4675

From Little Presque Isle to the southeast, a sandstone bluff rises up out of Lake Superior and sports two steep ice pillars that can be rapped into or in good years walk the lake ice from the Wetmore Landing parking lot.

Hidden Beach ☐
WI2 7 meters
N46.6216 W87.4667

These three short flows usually form later in the season and drop from the cliffline down towards Hidden Beach. A short snow slog leads to the ice on the upper section of the cliff.

Lakeshore Climb
Joseph Thill
Scott Crady

MARQUETTE COUNTY

Hogback Mountain

Hogback Mountain is a prominent peak that rises 600 feet above the surrounding terrain just to the north of Marquette. It is one of the southernmost peaks in the remote Huron Mountain Range that extends northwest to the Huron River more than 25 miles away. Most of the ice climbing found on Hogback is located at the base of the peak and is formed by snowmelt.

Directions

From downtown Marquette, follow the scenic Lake Shore Boulevard north. At the intersection with Haley Street turn left (Haley Street will turn into CR550). Drive 5.5 miles until you see the Sugarloaf Mountain sign on the right hand side of the road. .5 miles later on the lefthand side of the road is the Wetmore Pond trail head. Park on the side of CR550 as the parking lot is not plowed.

Wolf's Den ☐
WI3 8 meters
N46.6048 W87.4661

Looking for a quick pump right outside of Marquette? This short delicate sheet of ice is formed by snowmelt so it seems to be a better late season climb. The start is always thin and gets increasingly thicker towards the top. A mixed variation climbers left goes at M3/4.

The Grotto ☐
WI3 8 meters
N46.6040 W87.4893

Situated beneath Hogback Mountain, this climbing spot offers something for everyone. Climb the easy slab route in the middle or choose the steep ice for something more challenging. Looking to do a bit of mixed climbing? Climber's left of the Grotto a steep wall provides tiny holds and thin smears of ice.

Mini Mixed ☐
WI3 M4 7 meters N46.6039 W87.4897

Located near the cutoff trail to the Grotto, this fun little climb offers good drytool placements and thin ice in a remote setting.

The Grotto
Joe Thill ✗
Scott Crady 📷

Wolf's Den
Nic Dobbs
David Hixenbaugh

MARQUETTE COUNTY

Big Bay Area

23 miles north of Marquette, at the end of a dead end road, sits the sleepy town of Big Bay. A winter outdoor enthusiast's paradise, this two bar town is the jumping off point to some of the more remote climbs in the Upper Peninsula. Want to climb over a frozen Lake Superior? They've got that. Looking for a remote climb that might have had three ascents in 15 years? They have that too!

It's a perfect place to spend a day exploring with scenery that can't be beat and a feeling of wildness that's not often found. Plus, it's close enough to civilization that you can end your day enjoying a good meal and a better beer!

Scratch Wall
X David Hixenbaugh
📷 Bill Thompson

Burns Landing

When given the right conditions, the climbs along the cliffs of Burns Landing are a must do! Access can be tricky as the climbs are reached by walking on a frozen Lake Superior. The routes are located on the sandstone cliffs that run between Burns Landing and Black Rocks Cape. Some of the climbs listed below do not top out and trees are not always available so be prepared to utilize V threads to get down off of some of the routes.

To access the climbs take CR 550 north from Marquette to Big Bay. You will pass the historic Thunder Bay Inn and take the first right on KCB Road. Take the second left on KF Road towards the Marina. Go past the marina and you will come to a dead end, parking area for Burns Landing.

Crystal Clear ☐
WI3–4   12 meters
N46.8403 W87.7353

From the parking lot walk the lake ice north/northwest following the bluff. This climb is not visible from the parking area, but will come into view after a 15–20 minute hike: a nice steep curtain with a strip of clear ice right up the middle of the flow. Climb and top out on a ledge with small tree to rap off.

Crystal Clear
X David Hixenbaugh
📷 Erik Olsen

Diamond in the Rough ☐
WI3   18 meters
N46.8472 W87.7367

Follow the bluff passed *Crystal Clear* for another 10 minutes passing smaller flows/ seeps. The climb starts at a low angle sheet of ice gradually turning vertical at the finish. This climb stops abruptly three quarters of the way to the top of the cliff band. Be sure to have your V Thread skill handy to escape from the top!

Moonstone ☐
WI2–3   30 meters
N46.8491 W87.7363

This is the largest flow in the area and can be seen from the parking area at the end of KCB Road. From the trail head it is a 35-minute hike and is a sheet of ice that increases in steepness the higher you go. If conditions are cold and the ground is frozen, it is possible to climb to the top of the cliff by swinging into frozen mud and moss. Make a 30-meter rap off of the trees or V thread from the top of the ice 18–20 meters to the lake.

Diamond in the Rough
X David Hixenbaugh
📷 Erik Olsen

Lakeshore Approach
X David Hixenbaugh
📷 Erik Olsen

MARQUETTE COUNTY

Red Road

Red Road runs from County Road 510 in Ishpeming Township into the wild lands of the central Upper Peninsula. This area traditionally receives some of the largest concentrations of snow outside of the Keweenaw Peninsula, so snowshoes or skis are a must. Most of the climbs in this area are produced from snowmelt running over rock so if you are looking for an adventure it is best to explore this area later in the season to enable the climbs to form and build.

Directions

From Marquette, head north on County Road 550 for 22 miles toward Big Bay. A little ways after you pass Alder Creek you will see the T intersection sign declaring County Road 510 to the left. Take County Road 510 2.6 miles to the 510 / AAA intersection. 510 continues to the left and turns into dirt. Follow this for 21 miles to the intersection of the Red Road. Turn right and travel 1.75 miles to a small intersection with CR GGA. Turn right, cross the Boise Creek bridge. Two miles down this unimproved road the climbs will appear to the north (right hand side of the road) and visible through a clear cut.

Watch Tower
X David Hixenbaugh
📷 Bill Thompson

Watch Tower ☐
WI4   10 meters
N46.6520 W87.7160

As you approach the climb *Purple Haze*, up along the ridge to the north west you will see the top of *Watch Tower* peaking out above the trees. The 10-meter climb flows down over solid rock with the top being protected by a large bulbous section of ice. Several lines exist on the formation including on either side of the bulbous section.

Are You Experienced? ☐
WI3   28 meters   N46.6560 W87.7351

This is a beautiful flow of ice splitting two large cliff bands. The climb has multiple vertical steps separated by low angle sections. In certain years a more difficult sustained line forms on climbers right which may require mixed tactics. A 60-meter rope will just get you down from the trees at the top.

Purple Haze ☐
WI3   8 meters   N46.6510 W87.7114

Situated high above a clearcut, *Purple Haze* delivers a dreamy burst of euphoria during this short challenging climb.

Scratch Wall
WI3 6 meters
N46.7133 W87.7048

Smack in the middle of the Marquette "highlands", the *Scratch Wall* is one of the first climbs to form in the Upper Peninsula. Eager climbers who are itching to get out and start their season find their way out to CR 510 and mix climb on this formation. As the season progresses, the ice forms a large fat curtain perfect for first time climbers. The ice practically drops into the road so hands down the shortest approach in the U.P.

Travel CR 550 out of Marquette to CR 510 Turn left and travel down 510 until you see the ice formation on the right hand side of the road.

Scratch Wall
David Hixenbaugh
Bill Thompson

Are You Experienced?
Nic Dobbs
David Hixenbaugh

COPPER COUNTRY

The Keweenaw Peninsula is one of wildest and most overlooked places in country, so much so that it is commonly left off government maps. Little development and fewer people have made it a haven for those looking to get away from the crowds. It's often called "the last of the old U.P." and has a distinct character and charm that can't be found anywhere else.

Accessible climbs are primarily waterfalls flowing off of the basalt spine of the peninsula, where deep underground veins of copper set the stage for the nation's first mining boom. Rich deposits of native copper brought thousands of people to seek their fortunes underground but the expense of hard-rock mining and the discovery of more easily accessed ore led to the closing of the mines. Since the end of the copper mining era little has changed. The people still hold to their old ways as rugged individualism and self-reliance are defining characteristics of both the locals and the climbing.

**Lakeshore Ice
in the Keweenaw**
Abbie Bruns
John Morris

The defining feature of the peninsula is snow. Someone once said when it comes to snow, there's the Keweenaw, and then there is everywhere else. With an average snowfall of nearly 300 inches, you can expect every aspect of your adventure here to be impacted. Bring snowshoes or skis, drive a little slower because no one can see over the 10ft snowbanks, and be prepared to work a little harder for everything. Locally, it's called Michiganeering, you'll see why.

Many climbs exist in the area on private land or land with limited access. There are also a ton of climbs waiting to be discovered as the Keweenaw is relatively unexplored by anyone but the handful of local, tight lipped, climbers. If you make it to the end of the road, we ask that you respect local land owners and stay off private property, even if it contains the sweetest lines. With any luck access to these areas will open.

COPPER COUNTRY

Hungarian Falls

A public park in Tamarack City, this spot contains several small waterfalls and offers some fun, if short, climbs. A deep gorge creates a unique setting, and a popular trail network makes for easy access to the climbs. It's a great place to get in some laps in after work or take new climbers looking to test themselves on some easy, low commitment climbs.

Directions

Head north out of Houghton, take a right after crossing the Portage Lift Bridge and follow M26 east. In the small town of Tamarack City take a left on to 6th Street. Park on the side of the road at the bottom of the hill. Hike the seasonal road up to the gorge then follow the popular snowshoe trail to the main falls.

Main Falls ☐
WI2–3   18 meters
N47.1714 W88.4471

A large snow slope leads up to 10 meters of mellow climbing on this large waterfall. Anchors can be tricky as there are few trees at the top but it makes for a great place for the novice leader to hone their skills. Access via trails to the top or bottom.

Hidden Hungarian ☐
WI3   15 meters
N47.1709 W88.4470

Tucked away across the creek south of the *Main Falls* is this steeper climb. While less massive than the Main Falls, it offers much better climbing with a shorter snow slope and more vertical ice. To access, you can either cross the creek above the main falls and walk along the gorge, or cross at the snowmobile bridge and hike up the south side of the gorge.

Hidden Hungarian
Brian Wiesner ✕
Matt Abbotts 📷

Under the Bridge
WI3 6 meters N47.1691 W88.4407

Possibly the easiest access and quickest setup of any climb in the U.P. This short, steep piece of ice is great for quick laps when time is limited. Located under the south side of the snowmobile bridge it's a welcome find for any trolls venturing north.

Middle Falls
WI2 6 meters
N47.1721 W88.4478

Just upstream of the *Main Falls* is this short waterfall. Situated in a sandstone bowl, it gets fatter and easier the further into the season you get.

Upper Falls
WI2 7 meters
N47.1721 W88.4478

A small waterfall flowing over basalt, this very easy climb is a great place to introduce climbers to ice or just something to tick off the list.

Main Falls
Matt Abbotts
Hannah Abbotts

COPPER COUNTRY

Douglass Houghton Falls
Arni Ronis
Matt Abbotts

Douglass Houghton Falls
WI3+   40 meters
N47.2070 W88.4273

The tallest waterfall in Michigan, and likely one of the tallest in the Midwest, *Douglass Houghton Falls* offers a fun climb. The bottom is often buried under many feet of snow due to its low angle and it can be a real work out to gain the steeper ice near the top.

These falls were inaccessible for nearly 20 years due to private ownership, but are now in the process of becoming a Michigan scenic area and open to the public. At the time of printing this process is not finished so the falls are still off limits. Please call Down Wind Sports in Houghton (906-482-2500) for the current status.

WESTERN U.P.

A typical Western U.P. approach at Norwich
✗ :Jon Jugenheimer
📷 : Dave Rone

The wild west. A land of dense forests, small towns and remote ice. This area is a treasure trove for the modern day explorer. Spread out across the vastness of the state west of Houghton is a nearly unbroken tract of forest. Hidden among the trees are frozen waterfalls and ice-covered cliffs just waiting to be discovered.

You have to earn it out here. You won't find the easy approaches and convenient setups of Pictured Rocks. Long drives and grueling ski approaches lead to unforgettable climbs. Be prepared for deep snow, rugged terrain and virgin climbs. Don't expect packed trails, easy navigation or any people that could help you out when your car gets stuck in the deep snow. This is ice climbing at its best and is a true Yooper experience.

We've included all of the named climbs we could find (10 or so) but this is a land of a lot of ice and not a lot of people so there are many more climbs hidden in this forest. If you are feeling intrepid and are good with a map, this world is yours. Get out there, find some ice, have an experience, then let us know about it!

Houghton
Black River
Norwich Ledge
Marquette
Munising

WESTERN U.P.

A less typical Western U.P. approach at Black River
✗ Abbie Bruns
📷 John Morris

Black River

The Black is the Western U.P.'s mini ice destination in Big Snow Country, a region also known for its amount of alpine ski hills, and deep lake effect snow. The ice climbs are all located in a small canyon along the fast flowing Black River just a few miles upstream of where it drains into Lake Superior. On a normal season almost a half-dozen lines form along the sides of the canyon walls, with the actual river waterfall rarely freezing and never climbed. All but one of the climbs are located across the river from where you park, which means the river must be well frozen before you can get to the climbs, as the swim across would be rather cold.

Directions

Drive north from the town of Bessemer for exactly 14 miles to the parking area. Travel north on N. Moore street from US Hwy 2 in downtown Bessemer. Turn left onto Black River Road, also known as #513 for 13.75 miles to the Potawatomie and Gorge Falls parking area. The actual parking area is not plowed in winter, so park where it is plowed out along the road and then walk (usually tracked into the falls) along the road to the parking area and north to Gorge Falls. You can easily scout all the climbs from above the canyon, or simply drop down into the canyon following the wooden steps and boardwalk to get down to the river.

○ Black River

This river is fast moving, has deep pools, and sometimes doesn't freeze over until well after the ice climbs come into condition. To access all but one of the climbs, one must find a way across the river which is usually closer to *Mellow Yellow* than the main Gorge Falls, but the location of the thickest ice changes from year to year and day to day, including at times in the late season, blowing out completely with a fast thaw. Falling through the ice, and possibly being pulled under with a full pack of climbing gear could be fatal. So be safe and take our warning.

Pneumonia
Eric Landmann X
Erol Altay 📷

Pneumonia
WI4   20 meters   N46.6410 W90.0501

This is the only route on the same side of the river as the parking. It rarely forms, and if it does it is a late season climb. Located at the bottom of the stairs and overlook boardwalk, jump the fence at the bottom of the gorge and it will be on your left.

Mellow Yellow ☐
WI2   25 meters
N46.6405 W90.0500

This is the climb furthest downstream in the gorge, this mellow flow is the easiest in the canyon to get to the top of the gorge on the other side. Climb a rambling, low-angle flow up into the trees above, as this may be the easiest climb in the entire U.P.

Crystal Chandelier ☐
WI4+   16 meters
N46.6410 W90.0497

Located directly across the river from the viewing platform, *Crystal Chandelier* forms over the right margin of the largest cave in the gorge. Yellow ice pours from the trees above, into vertical curtain with a long ramp below. This is the other gem of the gorge, and should be on everyone's must do list.

Crystal Chandelier
X Erol Altay
📷 Eric Landmann

WESTERN U.P.

Paradise
Eric Landmann
Mike Chung

Crystal Chandelier
Gerry Voelliger ✘
John Morris 📷

Fallen Tree
WI4   20 meters
N46.6414 W90.0496

This seeping climb forms over a small cave later in the season. This route is similar to *Crystal Chandelier*, but doesn't form as consistently.

Paradise
WI4   25 meters
N46.6418 W90.0493

One of the two gems of the gorge, *Paradise* is a long, slender, vertical column of white ice that first catches your eye from the approach trail above on the opposite side of the canyon. With an ascent of this line, *Paradise* is found.

WESTERN U.P.

Book of Saturdays
Kim Hall
Jon Jugenheimer

Norwich Ledge

Situated in the far western Upper Peninsula, Norwich Ledge is about as "alpine" as you can get and true test of "Michiganeering". At 300 feet it is also the tallest cliff in the Midwest. The commiting nature of the climbing here makes it both a training ground for objectives further from home, or an destination in itself for someone wanting to test their winter climbing abilities. This is remote climbing and once you are on the wall you are far away from the car and civilization, and often on questionable rock.

Norwich is not a pure ice climbing destination, but rather a playground for traditional mixed climbing and a place for adventure. To date, the winter climbing style has been ground up and traditionally protected (within reason). Although bolting is currently an accepted practice for the area, grid bolting and sport routes are not. Please place as little fixed protection and as few belay bolts as possible when putting up new routes and or climbing existing routes with less ice present than on the FA.

The ledge is composed of volcanic rock called rhyolite, and goes from solid and compact to completely fractured choss in other areas, especially under roofs. The characteristics of the ledge are quite interesting as well, alternating roof and slab systems all the way to the top. The trick is to find a way around or over the roof systems and to follow the ice, if there is any.

Directions

From the town of Bergland, at the intersection of M28 and M64, travel north on M64 for two miles, then turn right on Old M64. In the next quarter of a mile, find a place off the road to park. Sometimes a resident plows a spot to sneak in your car for the day. Grab your skis and travel one mile of the road until it turns 90 degrees left (north). Be aware of snowmobiles on this road, keeping far right. At the turn, head straight for 50 feet to find the railroad tracks. Hit the tracks and turn left (north) for three more miles of travel. You will not be able to see the ledge until about two miles down the tracks. The ledge will be on the left (north) side of the tracks. Once you spot your route, turn into the woods from the tracks and head uphill until you are at the base of the ledge. 1.5–3 hours depending on fitness, snow depth and the size of your pack!

Descent

There is one bolted rappel route located on the climber's right side of the cliff. It is on the farthest vertical wall on the ledge, with the first anchor down from the top 15–20 meters. You can either rappel to the bottom in one 60 meter rappel, or stop at the half way anchor (currently a single bolt) and make it down in two rappels. Note, the top anchor will be buried under snow and will be very hard to onsite in those conditions. The other option is to rappel your climb.

Norwich Ledge
Jon Jugenheimer

WESTERN U.P.

Book of Saturdays
M5 80 meters
N46.6556 W89.5122

The *Book* is a summer rock route rated 5.9 and is the first known route on the face. It has two starts to it, but they both meet at the cave belay. In the winter, ice is found on the direct first pitch; whereas the final pitches are all on rock.

Pitch 1: Take the direct start of the route, going straight up a groove from below the cave. Belay on ice below and right of the cave. M3 30 meters

Pitch 2: From the belay, go back into the groove and ascend the chimney (crux, loose rock) and then into the cave. M5 10 meters

Pitch 3: Traverse left from the cave, behind a small tree and turn the corner onto the slab above. Climb the slab and corner into the trees above for the final belay.
M4 30 meters

Book of Saturdays
Jon Jugenheimer
Kim Hat

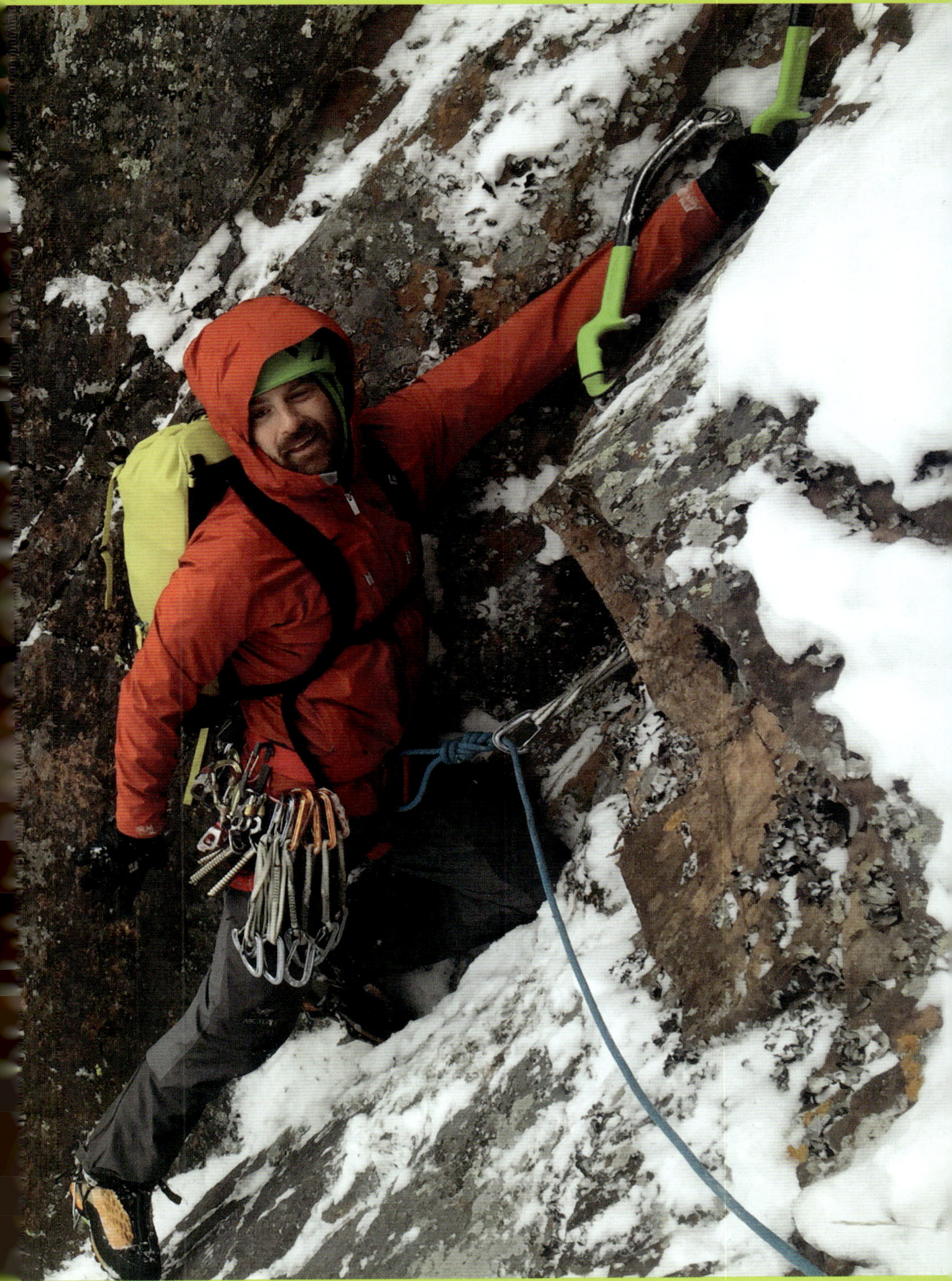

WESTERN U.P.

Parmotrema arnoldii
X Jon Jugeheimer
📷 Dave Rone

Parmotrema arnoldii
WI5–6 M7+ A0   80 meters   N46.6551 W89.5127

Parmotrema arnoldii is a type of lichen. Large, thick, disk-like flakes completely cover the crux pitch. These flakes are so large that they completely hide the rock edges, offering the illusion of security only to rip once a tool is pulled on. You will fully understand once you get there. Parmotrema is located about 150 meters left of Book of Saturday, under an obvious escape (the 4th pitch) through the highest series of roofs. Note that all of the pitches are relatively short, but required due to the traversing nature of the route.

Pitch 1: Start up a ramp to severely broken rock, aggressive cleaning was required on the FA. Climb up and left to under the roof. Gear is found above in a crack. Traverse up and left more to gain the ice and surmount the roof by turning to its side. Continue up and slightly left again following the crack in the slab. Belay at the single bolt that can be equalized with a pecker.

Pitch 2: Traverse right on the slab/foot ledge to the right-facing corner. Climb vertical WI5–6 ice to the top of the pillar. Set a hanging belay here off the screws.

Pitch 3: The FA traversed left around the corner utilizing a single bolt placed to gain the ice to climb above the roof. If possible, and in better style, climb the ice straight up and over the roof if present (it was not during the FA). Continue straight up the snow and verglas-covered slab to a wall above. Traverse right at the wall and around a corner and up a few more meters. Set a belay here. Screws were used on the FA.

Pitch 4: Climb right from the belay two meters, than straight up the horror show above. Use all your alpine trickery, shitty cams, pins, specters, nuts and a hope to get you up this pitch. Climb up the groove, to a small roof that leads in to the slot. Proceed up the slot (M7+) to just short of the top, escaping left when possible. 20 more meters of snow wallowing to the forest above leads to a belay on a large tree.

Parmotrema arnoldii
Dave Rone X
Jon Jugenheimer

WESTERN U.P.

Cheese Curd Gully
✗ Colten Moore
◉ Nic Dobbs

Cheese Curd Gully
WI3 M3   50 meters   N46.6556 W89.5122

Located on the far left side of the main cliff, this two pitch climb is noteworthy as having the potential of being most "in" of all of the routes on the ledge. Located in a gully, left of all of the known summer rock routes, this route is both the first to spot from the approach and the easiest way to the top of the cliff. The first ascent party rappelled the route.

Pitch 1: Start in a low-angle gully that eventually turns into a small left-facing dihedral with a few short rock moves to a small tree anchor on the left. M3 20 meters

Pitch 2: Follow the steepening gully past a few short vertical ice steps to the top of the gully. Belay off trees above. WI3 30 meters

White Rabbit
Colten Moore & Nic Dobbs
David Hixenbaugh

White Rabbit
WI3 M4   80 meters   N46.6533 W89.5195

This moderate climb is a great warm up for the other winter routes in the area. It is located on a separate, smaller cliff 5–10 minutes walk climber's left of the main walls.

Pitch 1: Start on easy mixed terrain at the base of a large slab in a right facing corner system. Pull some moves on rock and verglas heading towards the thicker ice higher in the corner. Traverse right toward a small alcove that makes a nice belay approximately 20 meters from the base. M4 20 meters

Pitch 2: From the belay head slightly right through steeper ground. As the angle eases off, follow the ice to the top of the wall. 2nd pitch is approx 30 meters to the trees. To descend, walk off to climbers right and follow the obvious gully down. WI3 M3 30 meters

Dairyland
✗ Ari Novak
📷 Jacob Raab

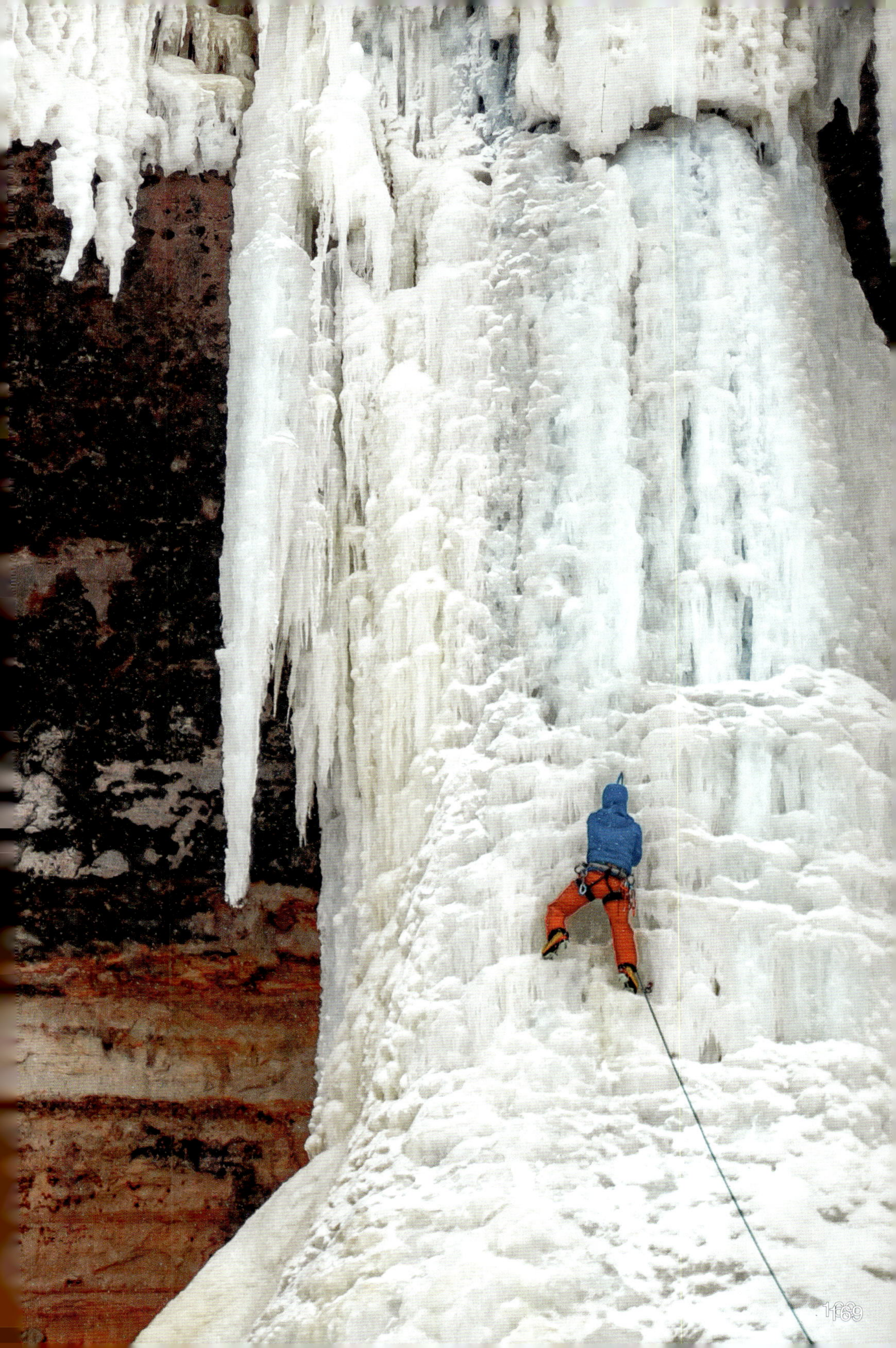

ROUTE INDEX

Route Name	Area	GPS	Grade	Height	Page	Tick
242	Grand Island West Shore	N46.5125 W86.7011	WI3	30m	119	☐
A Bone to Be Chewed	Grand Island North Shore	N46.5598 W86.6540	WI4	25m	131	☐
A Man and a Horse	Lakeshore Trail	N46.4680 W86.5812	WI4	13m	43	☐
A Walk In The Dark	Rock River Canyon	N46.3829 W86.9444	WI2	5m	136	☐
After Midnight	Mosquito to Chapel	N46.5507 W86.4564	WI5+	60m	75	☐
AGF	Inland	N46.4945 W86.5307	WI4	20m	89	☐
An Overhanging Wall	Mosquito to Chapel	N46.5296 W86.4915	WI6	20m	66	☐
Apocalypse Now	Grand Island Trout Bay	N46.5184 W86.6297	WI4+	45m	107	☐
April Ice is Nice	Lakeshore Trail	N46.4544 W86.5920	WI3	8m	39	☐
Are You Experienced?	Marquette County	N46.6560 W87.7351	WI3	28m	146	☐
Baby Blue	Grand Island North Shore	N46.5550 W86.6948	WI2+	10m	129	☐
Back Bowl	Grand Island West Shore	N46.5180 W86.7018	WI4	45m	122	☐
Bay View	Grand Island North Shore	N46.5578 W86.6584	WI4	20m	130	☐
Big Pine Pillar	Lakeshore Trail	N46.4493 W86.5968	WI3	7m	38	☐
Bird's Eye View	Grand Island West Shore	N46.5107 W86.7009	WI3	60m	118	☐
Black Rocks Bouldering	Marquette County	N46.5901 W87.3770	-	-	140	☐
BonaFide	Grand Island West Shore	N46.5080 W86.6989	WI4	70m	116	☐
Book Of Saturdays	Western U.P.	N46.6556 W89.5122	M5	80m	162	☐
Boomer Falls	Front Country	N46.4392 W86.6087	WI3	8m	30	☐
Boreas	Lakeshore Trail	N46.4852 W86.5589	WI4	20m	57	☐
Bourbon and Lemonade	Grand Island West Shore	N46.4757 W86.6861	WI3	20m	112	☐
Bridalveil Falls	Miner's to Mosquito	N46.5085 W86.5233	WI4	55m	62	☐
Broken Arrow	Grand Island West Shore	N46.5426 W86.7087	WI3	25m	125	☐
Brownie Surprise	East of Chapel Beach	N46.5589 W86.4077	WI4	18m	83	☐
Bulls on Parade	Mosquito to Chapel	N46.5466 W86.4734	WI4	40m	73	☐
Burl Falls	Inland	N46.4858 W86.5335	WI4	13m	89	☐
Burr on a Boat	Mosquito to Chapel	N46.5330 W86.4887	WI4	20m	66	☐
Calumet Girls	Lakeshore Trail	N46.4552 W86.5912	WI3	9m	39	☐
Candlestick Maker	Grand Island West Shore	N46.5283 W86.7040	WI5	35m	123	☐
Carny Creek	Grand Island West Shore	N46.5308 W86.7040	WI3	45m	124	☐
Cautiously Optimistic	Grand Island North Shore	N46.5506 W86.7011	WI4	30m	128	☐
Cedar Creek Falls	Grand Island West Shore	N46.5050 W86.6975	WI3	17m	115	☐
Certainly Dejected	Grand Island North Shore	N46.5502 W86.7018	WI4	30m	128	☐
Chapel Falls	Inland	N46.5287 W86.4441	WI2	30m	91	☐
Cheese Curd Gully	Western U.P.	N46.6540 W89.5155	WI3 M3	50m	167	☐
Chicken and Waffles	Grand Island West Shore	N46.4776 W86.6863	WI3	13m	113	☐
Chimp Simpleton	Mosquito to Chapel	N46.5455 W86.4770	WI5	30m	71	☐
Cork Screwed	East of Chapel Beach	N46.5592 W86.4071	WI4-	15m	83	☐
Cornbread Mafia	Grand Island West Shore	N46.4775 W86.6863	WI3	20m	113	☐
Crow	Rock River Canyon	N46.3849 W86.9415	WI3	6m	137	☐
Crystal Chandelier	Western U.P.	N46.6410 W90.0497	WI4+	16m	157	☐
Crystal Clear	Marquette County	N46.8403 W87.7353	WI3-4	12m	145	☐
Curtain Call	Front Country	N46.4388 W86.6094	WI3	7m	30	☐
Curtains II	Lakeshore Trail	N46.4814 W86.5639	WI4+	55m	55	☐
Dairyland	Lakeshore Trail	N46.4758 W86.5692	WI5	50m	50	☐

Route Name	Area	GPS	Grade	Height	Page	Tick
Dapper Dan	Grand Island West Shore	N46.5085 W86.6990	WI3+	65m	116	☐
Deadwood	Lakeshore Trail	N46.4844 W86.5597	WI4+	30m	57	☐
Diamond In the Rough	Marquette County	N46.8472 W87.7367	WI3	18m	145	☐
Douglass Houghton Falls	Copper Country	N47.2070 W88.4273	WI3+	40m	153	☐
Dragon Queen	Rock River Canyon	N46.3851 W86.9403	WI4	8m	137	☐
Drake Seep	Front Country	N46.4437 W86.6049	WI3	6m	33	☐
Dream Line	Mosquito to Chapel	N46.5412 W86.4821	WI5	45m	69	☐
Eagle View	Grand Island North Shore	N46.5518 W86.6990	WI4	23m	128	☐
East Channel Climbs	Grand Island East Channel	N46.4629 W86.6161	WI4	30m	97	☐
Eben Ice Caves	Rock River Canyon	N46.3828 W86.9445	WI3	6m	136	☐
El Lanzón	Lakeshore Trail	N46.4819 W86.5631	WI4	20m	56	☐
End Of the World	Grand Island Trout Bay	N46.5166 W86.6303	WI4	45m	106	☐
Fallen Feather	East of Chapel Beach	N46.5527 W86.4237	WI5+	25m	81	☐
Fallen Tree	Western U.P.	N46.6414 W90.0496	WI4	20m	159	☐
FFF	East of Chapel Beach	N46.5585 W86.4086	WI4	24m	80	☐
Final Act	Front Country	N46.4383 W86.6100	WI2	6m	30	☐
First Experience	Mosquito to Chapel	N46.5406 W86.4824	WI5	45m	69	☐
Fish Out of Water	Grand Island Trout Bay	N46.4842 W86.6206	WI5	18m	103	☐
Fists With Your Toes	Grand Island Trout Bay	N46.4848 W86.6209	WI3+	18m	103	☐
Flaming Stink Socks	Miner's to Mosquito	N46.4987 W86.5308	WI3	8m	60	☐
Foster Falls	Front Country	N46.4076 W86.6384	WI3	10m	28	☐
Fred Astaire	Mosquito to Chapel	N46.5491 W86.4489	WI3	30m	77	☐
Gales of November	Grand Island North Shore	N46.5597 W86.6542	WI3	25m	131	☐
George Carlin	Grand Island Trout Bay	N46.5165 W86.6303	WI4	45m	106	☐
Giddy Up	Lakeshore Trail	N46.4658 W86.5824	WI3	25m	42	☐
Ginger Rodgers	Mosquito to Chapel	N46.5487 W86.4475	WI3	30m	77	☐
Glad She's Fat	Grand Island Trout Bay	N46.4806 W86.6249	WI3	12m	102	☐
Grand Winterreise	Grand Island North Shore	N46.5589 W86.6554	WI4+	25m	130	☐
Gull Point Creek Falls	Grand Island North Shore	N46.5534 W86.6969	WI3–4	20m	129	☐
Gully Climb	Grand Island West Shore	N46.5095 W86.6995	WI2	48m	118	☐
Heart of Darkness	Grand Island Trout Bay	N46.5185 W86.6297	WI5	40m	107	☐
Hemlock Cascade	Inland	N46.4835 W86.5336	WI3	9m	89	☐
Hi Ho Silver	Lakeshore Trail	N46.4657 W86.5824	WI6	20m	42	☐
Hiawatha Falls	Grand Island West Shore	N46.5056 W86.6981	WI5	50m	115	☐
Hidden Beach	Marquette County	N46.6217 W87.4667	WI2	7m	141	☐
Hidden Hungarian	Copper Country	N47.1709 W88.4470	WI3	15m	150	☐
HMR	Mosquito to Chapel	N46.5507 W86.4565	WI5	60m	74	☐
Hook Line and Sinker	Grand Island Trout Bay	N46.4838 W86.6209	WI4	17m	103	☐
Hot Pepper Wall	Lakeshore Trail	N46.4847 W86.5594	WI3–4	18m	57	☐
Hungarian Main Falls	Copper Country	N47.1714 W88.4470	WI2–3	18m	150	☐
Hungarian Middle Falls	Copper Country	N47.1721 W88.4478	WI2	6m	151	☐
Hungarian Upper Falls	Copper Country	N47.1739 W88.4512	WI2	7m	151	☐
I Don't Know	Front Country	N46.4131 W86.6294	WI3	6m	28	☐
I See Your Point	Grand Island East Channel	N46.4917 W86.6095	WI3	25m	98	☐
I.O.U.s	Grand Island North Shore	N46.5452 W86.7080	WI3	25m	128	☐

ROUTE INDEX

Route Name	Area	GPS	Grade	Height	Page	Tick
I.O.U.s	Grand Island North Shore	N46.5452 W86.7080	WI3	25m	128	☐
Ice 10	Lakeshore Trail	N46.4560 W86.5904	WI3	6m	39	☐
Ice 9	Lakeshore Trail	N46.4556 W86.5907	WI3	9m	39	☐
Ice and Fire	Rock River Canyon	N46.3850 W86.9411	WI3	9m	137	☐
In Constant Sorrow	Grand Island West Shore	N46.5087 W86.6992	WI4	60m	117	☐
Intersection Falls	Lakeshore Trail	N46.4520 W86.5943	WI2	4m	38	☐
John Denver	Grand Island North Shore	N46.5458 W86.7071	WI3	25m	128	☐
Keep Dreaming	Mosquito to Chapel	N46.5418 W86.4821	WI5	45m	69	☐
Kemosabe	Lakeshore Trail	N46.4656 W86.5825	WI4+	16m	42	☐
Khione	Lakeshore Trail	N46.4852 W86.5588	WI4	18m	57	☐
Kind of Blue	Grand Island Trout Bay	N46.4819 W86.6230	WI3	7–10m	102	☐
Kokomo	Grand Island West Shore	N46.5121 W86.7012	WI3	30m	119	☐
Labyrinth	Lakeshore Trail	N46.4821 W86.5628	WI5	25m	56	☐
Lakeshore Climb	Marquette County	N46.6242 W87.4675	WI4	10m	141	☐
Lakeshore Curtains	Lakeshore Trail	N46.4533 W86.5931	WI3	6m	39	☐
Lap Dance	Grand Island Trout Bay	N46.4807 W86.6245	WI3	10m	102	☐
Leaning Tree	Grand Island West Shore	N46.5421 W86.7087	WI2	25m	125	☐

Caution and Adventure on Grand Island
X Arni Ronis
📷 Matt Abbotts

Route Name	Area	GPS	Grade	Height	Page	Tick
Left At the Altar	Miner's to Mosquito	N46.5086 W86.5230	WI4	30m	62	☐
Left Soda Straw	Lakeshore Trail	N46.4723 W86.5733	WI4+	25m	48	☐
Little Guy	East of Chapel Beach	N46.5581 W86.4095	WI3	20m	80	☐
Little One	Front Country	N46.4247 W86.6216	WI3	10m	29	☐
Mellow Yellow	Western U.P.	N46.6405 W90.0500	WI2	25m	157	☐
Memorial Falls	Front Country	N46.4175 W86.6271	WI3	10m	28	☐
Michigan Blue	Grand Island North Shore	N46.5525 W86.6982	WI4	25m	129	☐
Midnight Rambler	Lakeshore Trail	N46.4728 W86.5727	WI4	25m	49	☐
Miners Falls	Inland	N46.4748 W86.5319	WI4	15m	90	☐
Miners Lake Falls	Inland	N46.4805 W86.5323	WI3	18m	91	☐
Mini Me	Lakeshore Trail	N46.4692 W86.5788	WI3	7m	43	☐
Mini Mixed	Marquette County	N46.6039 W87.4897	WI3 M4	7m	142	☐
Mixed Masters	Mosquito to Chapel	N46.5473 W86.4718	WI5	40m	73	☐
Moonstone	Marquette County	N46.8491 W87.7363	WI2–3	30m	145	☐
Never Get Out of the Boat, Man.	Grand Island Trout Bay	N46.5185 W86.6296	WI3+	45m	107	☐
No Boundaries	Front Country	N46.4444 W86.6032	WI3	10m	33	☐
North Beach	Grand Island North Shore	N46.5585 W86.6565	WI3+	20m	130	☐
Oh George, Not the Cows	Grand Island West Shore	N46.5076 W86.6988	WI3	45m	116	☐
On The Rocks	Mosquito to Chapel	N46.5508 W86.4566	WI6	60m	75	☐
One Shot Mary Jane	Grand Island West Shore	N46.4758 W86.6861	WI3	20m	112	☐
Opening Curtain	Front Country	N46.4388 W86.6093	WI3	9m	30	☐
OverBite	Grand Island North Shore	N46.5584 W86.6857	WI4–5	40m	129	☐
Pack Down	Grand Island West Shore	N46.4762 W86.6861	WI4	22m	113	☐
Paradise	Western U.P.	N46.6418 W90.0493	WI4	25m	159	☐
Parmotrema arnoldii	Western U.P.	N46.6551 W89.5127	WI5-6 M7+	80m	165	☐
Paterfamilias	Grand Island West Shore	N46.5089 W86.6993	WI3	50m	117	☐
Peccadillo	Grand Island North Shore	N46.5594 W86.6549	WI3	20m	131	☐
Pillar of Pain	Grand Island West Shore	N46.5060 W86.6983	WI4	25m	115	☐
Pine Fresh	Grand Island West Shore	N46.4760 W86.6861	WI4	22m	112	☐
PK Special	Grand Island West Shore	N46.4756 W86.6861	WI4+	18m	112	☐
Pneumonia	Western U.P.	N46.6410 W90.0501	WI4	20m	157	☐
Potato Patch Falls	Miner's to Mosquito	N46.4989 W86.5302	WI3	10m	60	☐
Prelude Curtain	Front Country	N46.4385 W86.6098	WI3	7m	30	☐
Preservation Falls	Grand Island North Shore	N46.5554 W86.6926	WI3	25m	129	☐
Purple Haze	Lakeshore Trail	N46.4812 W86.5642	WI4+	55m	55	☐
Purple Haze	Marquette County	N46.6510 W87.7114	WI4+	55m	146	☐
R-U-N-N-O-F-T	Grand Island West Shore	N46.5082 W86.6990	WI3	60m	116	☐
Rabbit Hole	Grand Island West Shore	N46.5037 W86.6963	WI3	35m	114	☐
Rappin Ice	Lakeshore Trail	N46.4840 W86.5601	WI3	60m	56	☐
Resurrection	Mosquito to Chapel	N46.5452 W86.4774	WI6	35m	70	☐
Road to Nowhere	Miner's to Mosquito	N46.5105 W86.5203	WI4	40m	63	☐
Rock or Not	Front Country	N46.4132 W86.6293	WI3	10m	28	☐
Rock the Rabbit	Grand Island West Shore	N46.5033 W86.6959	WI4	35m	114	☐
Salmon of Capistrano	Grand Island North Shore	N46.5467 W86.7058	WI3	25m	128	☐
Sam Kinison	Grand Island Trout Bay	N46.5162 W86.6304	WI4	40m	106	☐

ROUTE INDEX

Route Name	Area	GPS	Grade	Height	Page	Tick
Sand Point Falls	Lakeshore Trail	N46.448 W86.5989	WI3	7m	38	☐
Schoolroom	Front Country	N46.4449 W86.6042	WI3	8m	34	☐
Scratch Wall	Marquette County	N46.7133 W87.7048	WI3	6m	147	☐
Sea Bass	Grand Island North Shore	N46.5476 W86.7047	WI3	25m	128	☐
Serial Bowl	Grand Island West Shore	N46.5236 W86.7031	WI3	45m	122	☐
Sheet of Ice	Lakeshore Trail	N46.4541 W86.5924	WI3	8m	39	☐
Ship's Prow	East of Chapel Beach	N46.5609 W86.4006	WI4	25m	85	☐
Shorts One And Two	Inland	N46.4953 W86.5306	WI3	5m	88	☐
Singing In Rain	Mosquito to Chapel	N46.5494 W86.4498	WI3	30m	76	☐
Snow Cone	Mosquito to Chapel	N46.5395 W86.4826	WI3+	40m	67	☐
Soggy Bottom Boys	Grand Island West Shore	N46.5079 W86.6988	WI3	50m	116	☐
Some Other Day	East of Chapel Beach	N46.5604 W86.4024	WI4	40m	84	☐
Soup or Bowl	Grand Island West Shore	N46.5197 W86.7028	WI3+	45m	122	☐
Spice World	Grand Island Trout Bay	N46.4809 W86.6243	WI2–3+	10m	102	☐
Spiral Staircase	Grand Island West Shore	N46.4756 W86.6861	WI5	15m	112	☐
Split Lip	Lakeshore Trail	N46.4809 W86.5645	WI5+	55m	54	☐
Spray Falls	East of Chapel Beach	N46.5579 W86.4105	WI4	25m	82	☐
Spray Off	Inland	N46.4747 W86.5319	WI4	10m	90	☐
Stairway to Heaven	Grand Island West Shore	N46.5065 W86.6988	WI4	50m	115	☐
State Fair	Grand Island West Shore	N46.5320 W86.7043	WI3–4	40m	124	☐
Steep Seep of 3	Lakeshore Trail	N46.4486 W86.5981	WI3	7m	38	☐
Strawberry Daze	Lakeshore Trail	N46.4811 W86.5644	WI4+	55m	54	☐
Suck It Up	Lakeshore Trail	N46.4706 W86.5767	WI4	20m	46	☐
Sugar Bush Falls	Inland	N46.4891 W86.5321	WI3	10m	89	☐
Sunny Day	Lakeshore Trail	N46.4694 W86.5786	WI2	15m	43	☐
Swamp Curtains	Lakeshore Trail	N46.4466 W86.5998	WI3	7m	38	☐
Swamp Thing	Lakeshore Trail	N46.4490 W86.5972	WI4	10m	38	☐
Sweet Mother Moses	Lakeshore Trail	N46.4617 W86.5856	WI4	23m	40	☐
Tannery Falls	Front Country	N46.4156 W86.6267	WI3	12m	28	☐
Teacher Says	Front Country	N46.4448 W86.6042	WI2	6m	34	☐
The Amphitheater	Front Country	N46.4427 W86.6059	WI5	20m	33	☐
The Art Of Seduction	Lakeshore Trail	N46.4546 W86.5919	WI3	10m	39	☐
The Balcony	Inland	N46.4962 W86.5307	WI3	7m	88	☐
The Butcher & The Baker	Grand Island West Shore	N46.5286 W86.7040	WI4-	40m	123	☐
The Chute	Mosquito to Chapel	N46.5341 W86.4869	WI3	20m	66	☐
The Curtain Climb	Lakeshore Trail	N46.4710 W86.5760	WI3	50m	46	☐
The Curtains	Front Country	N46.4396 W86.6082	WI3	10m	30	☐
The Dryer Hose	Front Country	N46.4407 W86.6066	WI4	23m	31	☐
The Freedom Years	East of Chapel Beach	N46.5596 W86.4044	WI4–5	15–45m	83	☐
The Good The Bad, & The Ugly	Lakeshore Trail	N46.4716 W86.5746	WI4	20m	47	☐
The Grotto	Inland	N46.4968 W86.5303	WI3	6m	88	☐
The Grotto	Marquette County	N46.6040 W87.4893	WI3	6m	142	☐
The Motherlode	Rock River Canyon	N46.3831 W86.9385	WI3	9m	136	☐
The One that Got Away	Grand Island Trout Bay	N46.4836 W86.6218	WI4	16m	103	☐
The Pencil	Mosquito to Chapel	N46.5387 W86.4825	WI6	40m	67	☐

Route Name	Area	GPS	Grade	Height	Page	Tick
The Portiére Area	Rock River Canyon	N46.3846 W86.9418	WI3	6m	137	☐
The Ramps	Grand Island Trout Bay	N46.5505 W86.6452	WI4–6	55m	109	☐
The Rim	Miner's to Mosquito	N46.5050 W86.5240	WI4	55m	61	☐
The Schooner	Grand Island West Shore	N46.5410 W86.7085	WI3-	25m	124	☐
The Seeping Wall	East of Chapel Beach	N46.5521 W86.4258	WI5	30m	80	☐
The Sloop	Grand Island West Shore	N46.5404 W86.7082	WI3-	25m	124	☐
The Steamer	Grand Island West Shore	N46.5406 W86.7083	WI3-	25m	124	☐
The Subway	Rock River Canyon	N46.3909 W87.0689	WI3	9m	137	☐
The Tug is the Drug	Grand Island Trout Bay	N46.4837 W86.6214	WI4	17m	103	☐
The Wall	Miner's to Mosquito	N46.5023 W86.5288	WI4	16m	61	☐
The White Line That Won	East of Chapel Beach	N46.5565 W86.4135	WI4	28m	82	☐
There Will Be Monsters	Lakeshore Trail	N46.4858 W86.5587	WI4	20m	57	☐
Thinly Sliced	Inland	N46.4979 W86.5304	WI3	7m	88	☐
Thousand Drips	Inland	N46.4965 W86.5306	WI3	5m	88	☐
Three Sisters	Lakeshore Trail	N46.4522 W86.5940	WI3	7m	38	☐
Three Stooges	Grand Island Trout Bay	N46.4806 W86.6253	WI3	11m	102	☐
Throwing out the Vibe	Grand Island North Shore	N46.5484 W86.7038	WI3	25m	128	☐
Tiger Country	Mosquito to Chapel	N46.5459 W86.4768	WI6	35m	71	☐
Totally Todd	Lakeshore Trail	N46.4538 W86.5927	WI3	8m	39	☐
Traverse of the Chickens	Mosquito to Chapel	N46.5454 W86.4772	WI4	50m	70	☐
Traverse of Tyrion	Rock River Canyon	N46.3849 W86.9391	-	-	137	☐
Tree Root	Grand Island West Shore	N46.4768 W86.6864	WI4	20m	113	☐
Trout Bay West Shore Curtains	Grand Island Trout Bay	N46.4937 W86.6446	WI3–6	10–55m	105	☐
Trout Point	Grand Island Trout Bay	N46.4938 W86.6115	WI3	10m	103	☐
Turf War	Marquette County	N46.5805 W87.3802	WI4	14m	140	☐
Turtle Power	Lakeshore Trail	N46.4703 W86.5776	WI4	13m	43	☐
Twilight	Mosquito to Chapel	N46.5471 W86.4726	WI4+	40m	73	☐
Twin Falls	Front Country	N46.4290 W86.6178	WI3	10m	29	☐
Twin Towers	Mosquito to Chapel	N46.5399 W86.4826	WI5-	45m	68	☐
Two Step	Grand Island North Shore	N46.5550 W86.6959	WI4	12m	129	☐
Udder Delight	Lakeshore Trail	N46.4764 W86.5684	WI5+	50m	53	☐
Under the Bridge	Copper Country	N47.1690 W88.4407	WI3	6m	151	☐
Use Your Polls	Grand Island West Shore	N46.5132 W86.7012	WI3	40m	119	☐
Watch Tower	Marquette County	N46.652 W87.716	WI4	10m	146	☐
West Road Seeps	Grand Island West Shore	N46.5355 W86.7061	WI2–4	30–40m	124	☐
West Shore Curtains	Grand Island West Shore	N46.5159 W86.7011	WI4	70m	120	☐
White Fang	East of Chapel Beach	N46.5580 W86.4100	WI6	20m	82	☐
Widow Maker	Inland	N46.4749 W86.5318	WI3	10m	90	☐
Wildlings	Rock River Canyon	N46.3848 W86.9419	WI3	6m	137	☐
Window Waltz	Front Country	N46.4176 W86.6270	WI3	7m	28	☐
Wish You Were Here	East of Chapel Beach	N46.5616 W86.3966	WI5	25m	85	☐
Wolf's Den	Marquette County	N46.6048 W87.4661	WI3	8m	142	☐
Y Climb	East of Chapel Beach	N46.5509 W86.4310	WI3	10m	80	☐
Yellow Curtains	Lakeshore Trail	N46.4755 W86.5698	WI5	30m	49	☐
Yooper Groove	Lakeshore Trail	N46.4780 W86.5665	WI4	17m	53	

Parmotrema arnoldii
✕ Jon Jugeheimer
📷 Dave Rone

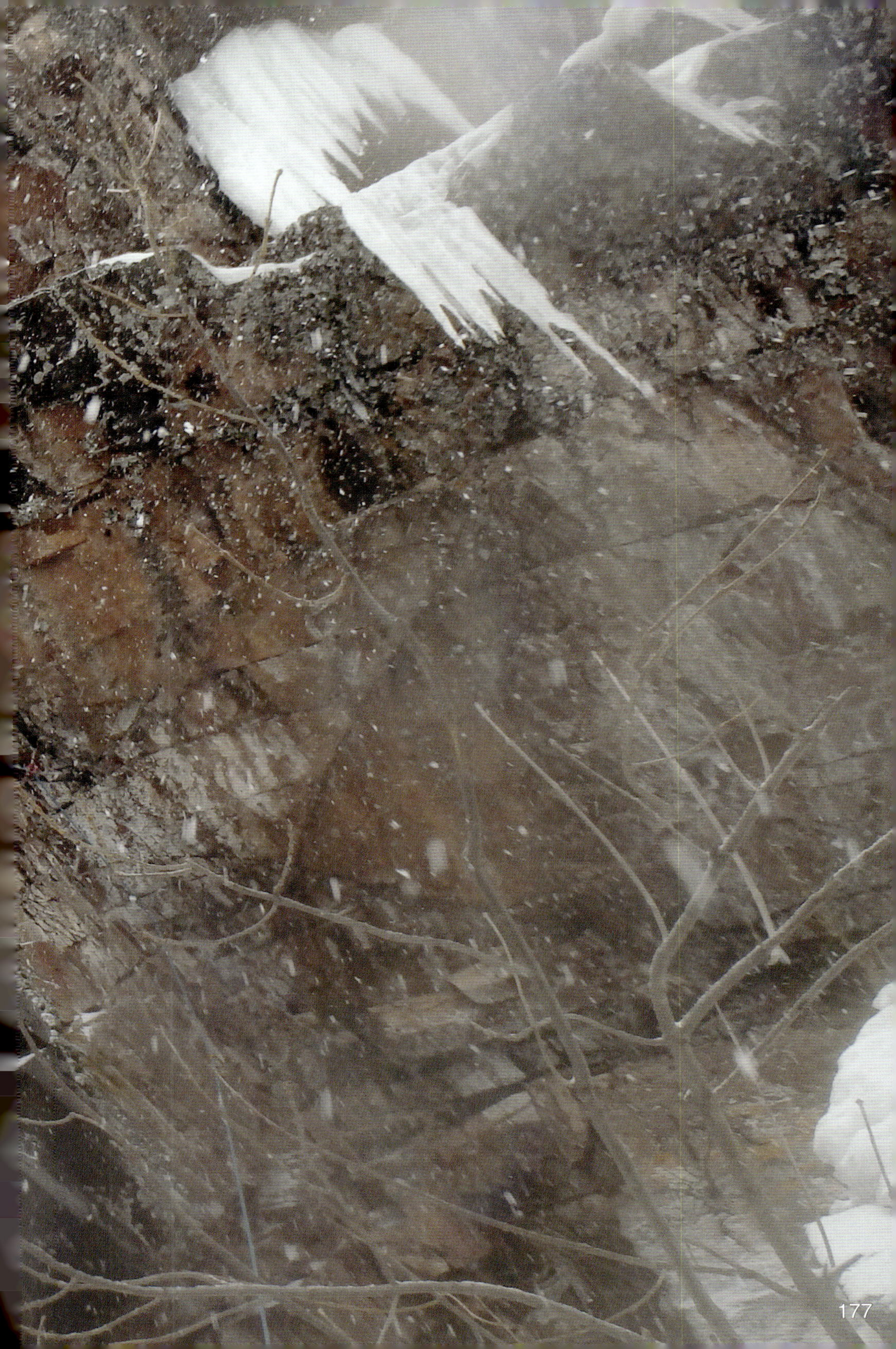

ROUTES BY GRADE

Route Name	Area	GPS	Grade	Height	Page	Tick
Black Rocks Bouldering	Marquette County	N46.5901 W87.3770	-	-	140	☐
Traverse of Tyrion	Rock River Canyon	N46.3849 W86.9391	-	-	137	☐
Cheese Curd Gully	Western U.P.	N46.6540 W89.5155	WI3 M3	50m	167	☐
Mini Mixed	Marquette County	N46.6039 W87.4897	WI3 M4	7m	142	☐
Book Of Saturdays	Western U.P.	N46.6556 W89.5122	M5	80m	162	☐
Parmotrema arnoldii	Western U.P.	N46.6551 W89.5127	WI5-6 M7+	80m	165	☐
A Walk In The Dark	Rock River Canyon	N46.3829 W86.9444	WI2	5m	136	☐
Chapel Falls	Inland	N46.5287 W86.4441	WI2	30m	91	☐
Final Act	Front Country	N46.4383 W86.6100	WI2	6m	30	☐
Gully Climb	Grand Island West Shore	N46.5095 W86.6995	WI2	48m	118	☐
Hidden Beach	Marquette County	N46.6217 W87.4667	WI2	7m	141	☐
Hungarian Middle Falls	Copper Country	N47.1721 W88.4478	WI2	6m	151	☐
Hungarian Upper Falls	Copper Country	N47.1739 W88.4512	WI2	7m	151	☐
Intersection Falls	Lakeshore Trail	N46.4520 W86.5943	WI2	4m	38	☐
Leaning Tree	Grand Island West Shore	N46.5421 W86.7087	WI2	25m	125	☐
Mellow Yellow	Western U.P.	N46.6405 W90.0500	WI2	25m	157	☐
Sunny Day	Lakeshore Trail	N46.4694 W86.5786	WI2	15m	43	☐
Teacher Says	Front Country	N46.4448 W86.6042	WI2	6m	34	☐
Baby Blue	Grand Island North Shore	N46.5550 W86.6948	WI2+	10m	129	☐
Hungarian Main Falls	Copper Country	N47.1714 W88.4470	WI2–3	18m	150	☐
Moonstone	Marquette County	N46.8491 W87.7363	WI2–3	30m	145	☐
Spice World	Grand Island Trout Bay	N46.4809 W86.6243	WI2–3+	10m	102	☐
West Road Seeps	Grand Island West Shore	N46.5355 W86.7061	WI2–4	30–40m	124	☐
The Schooner	Grand Island West Shore	N46.5410 W86.7085	WI3-	25m	124	☐
The Sloop	Grand Island West Shore	N46.5404 W86.7082	WI3-	25m	124	☐
The Steamer	Grand Island West Shore	N46.5406 W86.7083	WI3-	25m	124	☐
242	Grand Island West Shore	N46.5125 W86.7011	WI3	30m	119	☐
April Ice is Nice	Lakeshore Trail	N46.4544 W86.5920	WI3	8m	39	☐
Are You Experienced?	Marquette County	N46.6560 W87.7351	WI3	28m	146	☐
Big Pine Pillar	Lakeshore Trail	N46.4493 W86.5968	WI3	7m	38	☐
Bird's Eye View	Grand Island West Shore	N46.5107 W86.7009	WI3	60m	118	☐
Boomer Falls	Front Country	N46.4392 W86.6087	WI3	8m	30	☐
Bourbon and Lemonade	Grand Island West Shore	N46.4757 W86.6861	WI3	20m	112	☐
Broken Arrow	Grand Island West Shore	N46.5426 W86.7087	WI3	25m	125	☐
Calumet Girls	Lakeshore Trail	N46.4552 W86.5912	WI3	9m	39	☐
Carny Creek	Grand Island West Shore	N46.5308 W86.7040	WI3	45m	124	☐
Cedar Creek Falls	Grand Island West Shore	N46.5050 W86.6975	WI3	17m	115	☐
Chicken and Waffles	Grand Island West Shore	N46.4776 W86.6863	WI3	13m	113	☐
Cornbread Mafia	Grand Island West Shore	N46.4775 W86.6863	WI3	20m	113	☐
Crow	Rock River Canyon	N46.3849 W86.9415	WI3	6m	137	☐
Curtain Call	Front Country	N46.4388 W86.6094	WI3	7m	30	☐
Diamond In the Rough	Marquette County	N46.8472 W87.7367	WI3	18m	145	☐

HMR
Ari Novak ✕
Mike Wilkinson 📷

ROUTES BY GRADE

Route Name	Area	GPS	Grade	Height	Page	Tick
Drake Seep	Front Country	N46.4437 W86.6049	WI3	6m	33	☐
Eben Ice Caves	Rock River Canyon	N46.3828 W86.9445	WI3	6m	136	☐
Flaming Stink Socks	Miner's to Mosquito	N46.4987 W86.5308	WI3	8m	60	☐
Foster Falls	Front Country	N46.4076 W86.6384	WI3	10m	28	☐
Fred Astaire	Mosquito to Chapel	N46.5491 W86.4489	WI3	30m	77	☐
Gales of November	Grand Island North Shore	N46.5597 W86.6542	WI3	25m	131	☐
Giddy Up	Lakeshore Trail	N46.4658 W86.5824	WI3	25m	42	☐
Ginger Rodgers	Mosquito to Chapel	N46.5487 W86.4475	WI3	30m	77	☐
Glad She's Fat	Grand Island Trout Bay	N46.4806 W86.6249	WI3	12m	102	☐
Hemlock Cascade	Inland	N46.4835 W86.5336	WI3	9m	89	☐
Hidden Hungarian	Copper Country	N47.1709 W88.4470	WI3	15m	150	☐
I Don't Know	Front Country	N46.4131 W86.6294	WI3	6m	28	☐
I See Your Point	Grand Island East Channel	N46.4917 W86.6095	WI3	25m	98	☐
I.O.U.s	Grand Island North Shore	N46.5452 W86.7080	WI3	25m	128	☐
Ice 10	Lakeshore Trail	N46.4560 W86.5904	WI3	6m	39	☐
Ice 9	Lakeshore Trail	N46.4556 W86.5907	WI3	9m	39	☐
Ice and Fire	Rock River Canyon	N46.3850 W86.9411	WI3	9m	137	☐
John Denver	Grand Island North Shore	N46.5458 W86.7071	WI3	25m	128	☐
Kind of Blue	Grand Island Trout Bay	N46.4819 W86.6230	WI3	7–10m	102	☐
Kokomo	Grand Island West Shore	N46.5121 W86.7012	WI3	30m	119	☐
Lakeshore Curtains	Lakeshore Trail	N46.4533 W86.5931	WI3	6m	39	☐
Lap Dance	Grand Island Trout Bay	N46.4807 W86.6245	WI3	10m	102	☐
Little Guy	East of Chapel Beach	N46.5581 W86.4095	WI3	20m	80	☐
Little One	Front Country	N46.4247 W86.6216	WI3	10m	29	☐
Memorial Falls	Front Country	N46.4175 W86.6271	WI3	10m	28	☐
Miners Lake Falls	Inland	N46.4805 W86.5323	WI3	18m	91	☐
Mini Me	Lakeshore Trail	N46.4692 W86.5788	WI3	7m	43	☐
No Boundaries	Front Country	N46.4444 W86.6032	WI3	10m	33	☐
Oh George, Not the Cows	Grand Island West Shore	N46.5076 W86.6988	WI3	45m	116	☐
One Shot Mary Jane	Grand Island West Shore	N46.4758 W86.6861	WI3	20m	112	☐
Opening Curtain	Front Country	N46.4388 W86.6093	WI3	9m	30	☐
Paterfamilias	Grand Island West Shore	N46.5089 W86.6993	WI3	50m	117	☐
Peccadillo	Grand Island North Shore	N46.5594 W86.6549	WI3	20m	131	☐
Potato Patch Falls	Miner's to Mosquito	N46.4989 W86.5302	WI3	10m	60	☐
Prelude Curtain	Front Country	N46.4385 W86.6098	WI3	7m	30	☐
Preservation Falls	Grand Island North Shore	N46.5554 W86.6926	WI3	25m	129	☐
R-U-N-N-O-F-T	Grand Island West Shore	N46.5082 W86.6990	WI3	60m	116	☐
Rabbit Hole	Grand Island West Shore	N46.5037 W86.6963	WI3	35m	114	☐
Rappin Ice	Lakeshore Trail	N46.4840 W86.5601	WI3	60m	56	☐
Rock or Not	Front Country	N46.4132 W86.6293	WI3	10m	28	☐
Salmon of Capistrano	Grand Island North Shore	N46.5467 W86.7058	WI3	25m	128	☐
Sand Point Falls	Lakeshore Trail	N46.448 W86.5989	WI3	7m	38	☐
Schoolroom	Front Country	N46.4449 W86.6042	WI3	8m	34	☐
Scratch Wall	Marquette County	N46.7133 W87.7048	WI3	6m	147	☐
Sea Bass	Grand Island North Shore	N46.5476 W86.7047	WI3	25m	128	☐

Route Name	Area	GPS	Grade	Height	Page	Tick
Serial Bowl	Grand Island West Shore	N46.5236 W86.7031	WI3	45m	122	☐
Sheet of Ice	Lakeshore Trail	N46.4541 W86.5924	WI3	8m	39	☐
Shorts One And Two	Inland	N46.4953 W86.5306	WI3	5m	88	☐
Singing In Rain	Mosquito to Chapel	N46.5494 W86.4498	WI3	30m	76	☐
Soggy Bottom Boys	Grand Island West Shore	N46.5079 W86.6988	WI3	50m	116	☐
Steep Seep of 3	Lakeshore Trail	N46.4486 W86.5981	WI3	7m	38	☐
Sugar Bush Falls	Inland	N46.4891 W86.5321	WI3	10m	89	☐
Swamp Curtains	Lakeshore Trail	N46.4466 W86.5998	WI3	7m	38	☐
Tannery Falls	Front Country	N46.4156 W86.6267	WI3	12m	28	☐
The Art Of Seduction	Lakeshore Trail	N46.4546 W86.5919	WI3	10m	39	☐
The Balcony	Inland	N46.4962 W86.5307	WI3	7m	88	☐
The Chute	Mosquito to Chapel	N46.5341 W86.4869	WI3	20m	66	☐
The Curtains	Front Country	N46.4396 W86.6082	WI3	10m	30	☐
The Curtain Climb	Lakeshore Trail	N46.4710 W86.5760	WI3	50m	46	☐
The Grotto	Inland	N46.4968 W86.5303	WI3	6m	88	☐
The Grotto	Marquette County	N46.6040 W87.4893	WI3	6m	142	☐
The Motherlode	Rock River Canyon	N46.3831 W86.9385	WI3	9m	136	☐
The Portiére Area	Rock River Canyon	N46.3846 W86.9418	WI3	6m	137	☐
The Subway	Rock River Canyon	N46.3909 W87.0689	WI3	9m	137	☐
Thinly Sliced	Inland	N46.4979 W86.5304	WI3	7m	88	☐
Thousand Drips	Inland	N46.4965 W86.5306	WI3	5m	88	☐
Three Sisters	Lakeshore Trail	N46.4522 W86.5940	WI3	7m	38	☐
Three Stooges	Grand Island Trout Bay	N46.4806 W86.6253	WI3	11m	102	☐
Throwing out the Vibe	Grand Island North Shore	N46.5484 W86.7038	WI3	25m	128	☐
Totally Todd	Lakeshore Trail	N46.4538 W86.5927	WI3	8m	39	☐
Trout Point	Grand Island Trout Bay	N46.4938 W86.6115	WI3	10m	103	☐
Twin Falls	Front Country	N46.4290 W86.6178	WI3	10m	29	☐
Under the Bridge	Copper Country	N47.1690 W88.4407	WI3	6m	151	☐
Use Your Polls	Grand Island West Shore	N46.5132 W86.7012	WI3	40m	119	☐
Widow Maker	Inland	N46.4749 W86.5318	WI3	10m	90	☐
Wildlings	Rock River Canyon	N46.3848 W86.9419	WI3	6m	137	☐
Window Waltz	Front Country	N46.4176 W86.6270	WI3	7m	28	☐
Wolf's Den	Marquette County	N46.6048 W87.4661	WI3	8m	142	☐
Y Climb	East of Chapel Beach	N46.5509 W86.4310	WI3	10m	80	☐
Dapper Dan	Grand Island West Shore	N46.5085 W86.6990	WI3+	65m	116	☐
Douglass Houghton Falls	Copper Country	N47.2070 W88.4273	WI3+	40m	153	☐
Fists With Your Toes	Grand Island Trout Bay	N46.4848 W86.6209	WI3+	18m	103	☐
Never Get Out of the Boat, Man.	Grand Island Trout Bay	N46.5185 W86.6296	WI3+	45m	107	☐
North Beach	Grand Island North Shore	N46.5585 W86.6565	WI3+	20m	130	☐
Snow Cone	Mosquito to Chapel	N46.5395 W86.4826	WI3+	40m	67	☐
Soup or Bowl	Grand Island West Shore	N46.5197 W86.7028	WI3+	45m	122	☐
Crystal Clear	Marquette County	N46.8403 W87.7353	WI3–4	12m	145	☐
Gull Point Creek Falls	Grand Island North Shore	N46.5534 W86.6969	WI3–4	20m	129	☐
Hot Pepper Wall	Lakeshore Trail	N46.4847 W86.5594	WI3–4	18m	57	☐

ROUTES BY GRADE

Route Name	Area	GPS	Grade	Height	Page	Tick
State Fair	Grand Island West Shore	N46.5320 W86.7043	WI3–4	40m	124	☐
Trout Bay West Shore Curtains	Grand Island Trout Bay	N46.4937 W86.6446	WI3–6	10–55m	105	☐
Cork Screwed	East of Chapel Beach	N46.5592 W86.4071	WI4-	15m	83	☐
The Butcher & The Baker	Grand Island West Shore	N46.5286 W86.7040	WI4-	40m	123	☐
A Bone to Be Chewed	Grand Island North Shore	N46.5598 W86.6540	WI4	25m	131	☐
A Man and a Horse	Lakeshore Trail	N46.4680 W86.5812	WI4	13m	43	☐
AGF	Inland	N46.4945 W86.5307	WI4	20m	89	☐
Back Bowl	Grand Island West Shore	N46.5180 W86.7018	WI4	45m	122	☐
Bay View	Grand Island North Shore	N46.5578 W86.6584	WI4	20m	130	☐
BonaFide	Grand Island West Shore	N46.5080 W86.6989	WI4	70m	116	☐
Boreas	Lakeshore Trail	N46.4852 W86.5589	WI4	20m	57	☐
Bridalveil Falls	Miner's to Mosquito	N46.5085 W86.5233	WI4	55m	62	☐
Brownie Surprise	East of Chapel Beach	N46.5589 W86.4077	WI4	18m	83	☐
Bulls on Parade	Mosquito to Chapel	N46.5466 W86.4734	WI4	40m	73	☐
Burl Falls	Inland	N46.4858 W86.5335	WI4	13m	89	☐
Burr on a Boat	Mosquito to Chapel	N46.5330 W86.4887	WI4	20m	66	☐
Cautiously Optimistic	Grand Island North Shore	N46.5506 W86.7011	WI4	30m	128	☐
Certainly Dejected	Grand Island North Shore	N46.5502 W86.7018	WI4	30m	128	☐
Dragon Queen	Rock River Canyon	N46.3851 W86.9403	WI4	8m	137	☐
Eagle View	Grand Island North Shore	N46.5518 W86.6990	WI4	23m	128	☐
East Channel Climbs	Grand Island East Channel	N46.4629 W86.6161	WI4	30m	97	☐
El Lanzón	Lakeshore Trail	N46.4819 W86.5631	WI4	20m	56	☐
End Of the World	Grand Island Trout Bay	N46.5166 W86.6303	WI4	45m	106	☐
Fallen Tree	Western U.P.	N46.6414 W90.0496	WI4	20m	159	☐
FFF	East of Chapel Beach	N46.5585 W86.4086	WI4	24m	80	☐
George Carlin	Grand Island Trout Bay	N46.5165 W86.6303	WI4	45m	106	☐
Hook Line and Sinker	Grand Island Trout Bay	N46.4838 W86.6209	WI4	17m	103	☐
In Constant Sorrow	Grand Island West Shore	N46.5087 W86.6992	WI4	60m	117	☐
Khione	Lakeshore Trail	N46.4852 W86.5588	WI4	18m	57	☐
Lakeshore Climb	Marquette County	N46.6242 W87.4675	WI4	10m	141	☐
Left At the Altar	Miner's to Mosquito	N46.5086 W86.5230	WI4	30m	62	☐
Michigan Blue	Grand Island North Shore	N46.5525 W86.6982	WI4	25m	129	☐
Midnight Rambler	Lakeshore Trail	N46.4728 W86.5727	WI4	25m	49	☐
Miners Falls	Inland	N46.4748 W86.5319	WI4	15m	90	☐
Pack Down	Grand Island West Shore	N46.4762 W86.6861	WI4	22m	113	☐
Paradise	Western U.P.	N46.6418 W90.0493	WI4	25m	159	☐
Pillar of Pain	Grand Island West Shore	N46.5060 W86.6983	WI4	25m	115	☐
Pine Fresh	Grand Island West Shore	N46.4760 W86.6861	WI4	22m	112	☐
Pneumonia	Western U.P.	N46.6410 W90.0501	WI4	20m	157	☐
Road to Nowhere	Miner's to Mosquito	N46.5105 W86.5203	WI4	40m	63	☐
Rock the Rabbit	Grand Island West Shore	N46.5033 W86.6959	WI4	35m	114	☐
Sam Kinison	Grand Island Trout Bay	N46.5162 W86.6304	WI4	40m	106	☐
Ship's Prow	East of Chapel Beach	N46.5609 W86.4006	WI4	25m	85	☐
Some Other Day	East of Chapel Beach	N46.5604 W86.4024	WI4	40m	84	☐

Approach on the Lake Ice
Erik Olsen

ROUTES BY GRADE

Route Name	Area	GPS	Grade	Height	Page	Tick
Spray Falls	East of Chapel Beach	N46.5579 W86.4105	WI4	25m	82	☐
Spray Off	Inland	N46.4747 W86.5319	WI4	10m	90	☐
Stairway to Heaven	Grand Island West Shore	N46.5065 W86.6988	WI4	50m	115	☐
Suck It Up	Lakeshore Trail	N46.4706 W86.5767	WI4	20m	46	☐
Swamp Thing	Lakeshore Trail	N46.4490 W86.5972	WI4	10m	38	☐
Sweet Mother Moses	Lakeshore Trail	N46.4617 W86.5856	WI4	23m	40	☐
The Dryer Hose	Front Country	N46.4407 W86.6066	WI4	23m	31	☐
The Good The Bad, & The Ugly	Lakeshore Trail	N46.4716 W86.5746	WI4	20m	47	☐
The One that Got Away	Grand Island Trout Bay	N46.4836 W86.6218	WI4	16m	103	☐
The Rim	Miner's to Mosquito	N46.5050 W86.5240	WI4	55m	61	☐
The Tug is the Drug	Grand Island Trout Bay	N46.4837 W86.6214	WI4	17m	103	☐
The Wall	Miner's to Mosquito	N46.5023 W86.5288	WI4	16m	61	☐
The White Line That Won	East of Chapel Beach	N46.5565 W86.4135	WI4	28m	82	☐
There Will Be Monsters	Lakeshore Trail	N46.4858 W86.5587	WI4	20m	57	☐
Traverse of the Chickens	Mosquito to Chapel	N46.5454 W86.4772	WI4	50m	70	☐
Tree Root	Grand Island West Shore	N46.4768 W86.6864	WI4	20m	113	☐
Turf War	Marquette County	N46.5805 W87.3802	WI4	14m	140	☐
Turtle Power	Lakeshore Trail	N46.4703 W86.5776	WI4	13m	43	☐
Two Step	Grand Island North Shore	N46.5550 W86.6959	WI4	12m	129	☐
Watch Tower	Marquette County	N46.652 W87.716	WI4	10m	146	☐
West Shore Curtains	Grand Island West Shore	N46.5159 W86.7011	WI4	70m	120	☐
Yooper Groove	Lakeshore Trail	N46.4780 W86.5665	WI4	17m	53	☐
Apocalypse Now	Grand Island Trout Bay	N46.5184 W86.6297	WI4+	45m	107	☐
Crystal Chandelier	Western U.P.	N46.6410 W90.0497	WI4+	16m	157	☐
Curtains II	Lakeshore Trail	N46.4814 W86.5639	WI4+	55m	55	☐
Deadwood	Lakeshore Trail	N46.4844 W86.5597	WI4+	30m	57	☐
Grand Winterreise	Grand Island North Shore	N46.5589 W86.6554	WI4+	25m	130	☐
Kemosabe	Lakeshore Trail	N46.4656 W86.5825	WI4+	16m	42	☐
Left Soda Straw	Lakeshore Trail	N46.4723 W86.5733	WI4+	25m	48	☐
PK Special	Grand Island West Shore	N46.4756 W86.6861	WI4+	18m	112	☐
Purple Haze	Lakeshore Trail	N46.4812 W86.5642	WI4+	55m	55	☐
Purple Haze	Marquette County	N46.6510 W87.7114	WI4+	55m	146	☐
Strawberry Daze	Lakeshore Trail	N46.4811 W86.5644	WI4+	55m	54	☐
Twilight	Mosquito to Chapel	N46.5471 W86.4726	WI4+	40m	73	☐
OverBite	Grand Island North Shore	N46.5584 W86.6857	WI4–5	40m	129	☐
The Freedom Years	East of Chapel Beach	N46.5596 W86.4044	WI4–5	15–45m	83	☐
The Ramps	Grand Island Trout Bay	N46.5505 W86.6452	WI4–6	55m	109	☐
Twin Towers	Mosquito to Chapel	N46.5399 W86.4826	WI5-	45m	68	☐
Candlestick Maker	Grand Island West Shore	N46.5283 W86.7040	WI5	35m	123	☐
Chimp Simpleton	Mosquito to Chapel	N46.5455 W86.4770	WI5	30m	71	☐
Dairyland	Lakeshore Trail	N46.4758 W86.5692	WI5	50m	50	☐
Dream Line	Mosquito to Chapel	N46.5412 W86.4821	WI5	45m	69	☐

Route Name	Area	GPS	Grade	Height	Page	Tick
First Experience	Mosquito to Chapel	N46.5406 W86.4824	WI5	45m	69	☐
Fish Out of Water	Grand Island Trout Bay	N46.4842 W86.6206	WI5	18m	103	☐
Heart of Darkness	Grand Island Trout Bay	N46.5185 W86.6297	WI5	40m	107	☐
Hiawatha Falls	Grand Island West Shore	N46.5056 W86.6981	WI5	50m	115	☐
HMR	Mosquito to Chapel	N46.5507 W86.4565	WI5	60m	74	☐
Keep Dreaming	Mosquito to Chapel	N46.5418 W86.4821	WI5	45m	69	☐
Labyrinth	Lakeshore Trail	N46.4821 W86.5628	WI5	25m	56	☐
Mixed Masters	Mosquito to Chapel	N46.5473 W86.4718	WI5	40m	73	☐
Spiral Staircase	Grand Island West Shore	N46.4756 W86.6861	WI5	15m	112	☐
The Amphitheater	Front Country	N46.4427 W86.6059	WI5	20m	33	☐
The Seeping Wall	East of Chapel Beach	N46.5521 W86.4258	WI5	30m	80	☐
Wish You Were Here	East of Chapel Beach	N46.5616 W86.3966	WI5	25m	85	☐
Yellow Curtains	Lakeshore Trail	N46.4755 W86.5698	WI5	30m	49	☐
After Midnight	Mosquito to Chapel	N46.5507 W86.4564	WI5+	60m	75	☐
Fallen Feather	East of Chapel Beach	N46.5527 W86.4237	WI5+	25m	81	☐
Split Lip	Lakeshore Trail	N46.4809 W86.5645	WI5+	55m	54	☐
Udder Delight	Lakeshore Trail	N46.4764 W86.5684	WI5+	50m	53	☐
Amazing Pillar Area	Grand Island Trout Bay	N46.5260 W86.6289	WI5–6	30–55m	108	☐
An Overhanging Wall	Mosquito to Chapel	N46.5296 W86.4915	WI6	20m	66	☐
Hi Ho Silver	Lakeshore Trail	N46.4657 W86.5824	WI6	20m	42	☐
On The Rocks	Mosquito to Chapel	N46.5508 W86.4566	WI6	60m	75	☐
Resurrection	Mosquito to Chapel	N46.5452 W86.4774	WI6	35m	70	☐
The Pencil	Mosquito to Chapel	N46.5387 W86.4825	WI6	40m	67	☐
Tiger Country	Mosquito to Chapel	N46.5459 W86.4768	WI6	35m	71	☐
White Fang	East of Chapel Beach	N46.5580 W86.4100	WI6	20m	82	☐

Rappelling into the unknown
X Nic Dobbs
📷 Aaron Peterson

PHOTOGRAPHERS

If you think a picture is worth is a thousand words then the amazing photographers who helped out by providing photos for this guidebook wrote a lot more than the authors. Without their hard work we wouldn't have been able to complete the project. We can't thank them enough.

In Order of appearance, not order of importance. Thank you all.

Keith Ladzinski
Jason Gebauer
Paul Kuenn
Erik Olsen
Michael Soule
Joe Stylos
Scott Crady
Mario Molin
Bryan DeAugustine
Karsten Delap
Jack Frost
Jake Bourdow
John Morris
Dave Rone
Eric Landmann
Kim Hall
Mike Wilkinson
Max Lowe
Michael Tokarz
Jacob Rabb
Aaron Peterson
Linda Wappner
Nic Dobbs
Doug Hemken
Alex Schutzkus
Andrew Burr
Emily Oppliger
David Hixenbaugh
Hannah Abbotts
Erol Altay
Mike Chung

Mike Wilkinson climbing out after a long day of shooting.
Jon Jugenheimer

SPECIAL THANKS

This guidebook is not the work of just three people; this guidebook is the work of the entire community of ice climbers that gravitate around Munising Michigan and the Upper Peninsula. Without the community, the ice here would never have been climbed, The Michigan Ice Fest would never take place and you would not be a better person for having had the experiences only found here.

That being said, there are certain people that contributed to this guide, and without them it wouldn't be as good as it possibly could be. Without their generous offerings of photographs, beta, climbing partners and willingness to pay for a half a tank of gas to get here, this guidebook would have never been possible. I am sure that we have left off a name or two, and please accept our sincere apologies for that.

THANK YOU

Hannah Abbotts • Isla Abbotts • Andy Albosta • Erol Altay
Conrad Anker • Abbie Bruns • Andrew Burr
Ramsey and Cori Cearley • Cherryland Snowmobile Rentals
Scott Crady • Mike Chung • Peggy Cromwell • Adam Dailey
Bryan DeAugustine • Nic Dobbs • Robert Drake • Sam Elias
Kim Hall • David Hixenbaugh • Paul Kuenn • Jude Kuenn
Keith Ladzinski • Eric Landmann • Bryan Larue Liz Layne
James Loveridge • Max Lowe • MacGillivray Freeman Films
Andy Mann • Kate McKinstry Mario Molin • Colten Moore •
John Morris Joe Mucci • Amber Munoz • Murf • Brian Nation
Ari Novak • Erik Olsen Emily Oppliger • Garret Peabody
Aaron Peterson • Pictured Rocks National Lakeshore staff
Eric Pueschel • Jacob Raab • Bill Ramsey • Andrew Ranville
Mark Reisch Red Bull Media • Dave Riggs • Dave Rone • Arni Ronis
Heath Rowland • Joseph Schlitz • Raphael Slawinski
Bill Smith • Dave Sprygada • Kendra Stritch • Joe Stylos
The Michigan Ice Film produced by Clear & Cold Cinema
Lou Terzaghi • Joseph Thill • Blake Thompson
Yumi Thompson • Angela Vanwiemeersch • Gina Vendola
Gerry Voelliger • Linda Wappner • Phil Watts • Mark Wilford
Mike Wilkinson

THE AUTHORS

Jon Jugenheimer

Growing up in Madison, Wisconsin, ice climbing was not a childhood sport option for Jon. It took a frigid winter trip to the now defunct Ice Pit in Green Bay when he was 18 to be first introduced to the sport. He climbed 15 feet, got lowered off and was too pumped to untie his knot. He fell in love with ice climbing at that very moment.

That was 20 years ago and he has been climbing ice ever since. He has always considered Munising his home for winter climbing, as that was the place he truly learned to climb ice. His hope is that you will love the lakeshore as much as he does and to find adventure there with the help of this guidebook.

Bill Thompson

For the last 35 years, Bill has been fortunate enough to call the Upper Peninsula his home. After he graduated from Northern Michigan University with a Masters degree in Community College Teaching/Outdoor Recreation, he began a career at Down Wind Sports, an outdoor specialty retailer based in Marquette. In the summer Bill can usually be found rock climbing at the local crags, or paddling the shores of Lake Superior. It is when the north wind blows and the snow begins to fly that Bill follows his true passion — ice climbing. He is the organizer of the Michigan Ice Fest, is the chairperson for the Great Lakes Section of the American Alpine Club, and is a board member of the Upper Peninsula Climbers Coalition, an organization dedicated to preserving climbing areas in the U.P.

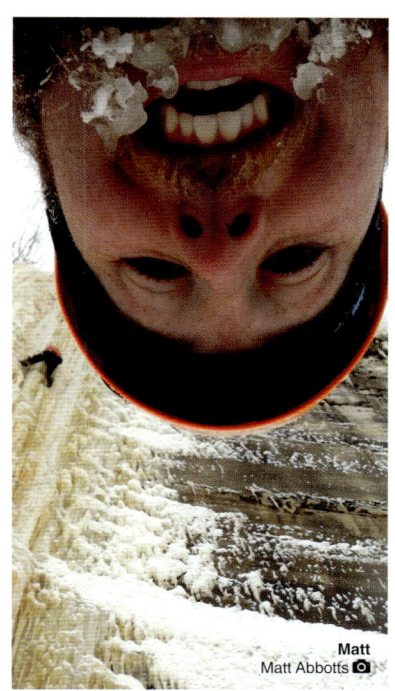

Matt Abbotts

Born in the flatlands of Central Michigan, Matt followed the compass north after he graduated high school and found paradise in Michigan's Keweenaw Peninsula. He fell in love with all things outdoors while studying forestry at Michigan Tech.

His first experience on ice was hitchhiking to the 2008 Michigan Ice Fest. One swing was all it took and seven years later he found himself one of the event's co-organizers.

A jack of all trades, and certainly a master of none, he splits his time between climbing, kayaking, fly fishing, trail running and pretty much anything else that keeps him outside.

Lately his passion has shifted to sharing his love of nature and wild places with his daughter Isla.

Matt
Matt Abbotts

The Authors and Arni Ronis during the Michigan Ice Fest
Unkonwn

NOTES

SIC ADVENTURES

SUPERIORICECLIMBINGADVENTURES.COM

906.399.8454

MUNISING, MICHIGAN

Angela VanWiemeersch climbs "HMR" above Lake Superior in Northern Michigan - Photo: Mike Wilkinson

GRIVEL

G20 PLUS
CRAMPON

REPLACABLE FRONT POINT
Better angle for gripping ice

TWO ADDITIONAL POINTS ADDED
More security and versatility

LOCAL RETAILER

DOWN WIND SPORTS - MARQUETTE | 514 N. THIRD ST. | 906-226-7112

Your gateway to the Pictured Rocks

The Pictured Rocks is comprised of over 15 miles of shoreline along Lake Superior and features hundreds of miles of scenic trails towering sandstone cliffs, countless waterfalls and lake views that will take your breath away. Visitors will experience forests, streams, shoreline, wildlife and so much more, and the city of Munising is the gateway to it all. With all of the ammenities you need for a memorable vacation including lodging, food, shopping, attractions, and events, Munising is the perfect place to relax, explore and enjoy the Pictured Rocks area.

Visit www.munising.org to learn more and start planning your Pictured Rocks vacation today.

MUNISING
Picture Perfect.

NOMIC & ERGONOMIC

Steep and steeper.

The new NOMIC maintains its world-famous swing and excels at climbing steep ice. Crafted for swinging and hooking into delicate or mixed lines, the ERGONOMIC is the choice for those climbing steeper or overhanging terrain. Both tools feature an overmolded dual handle, adjustable GRIPREST, modular head, and hydroformed shaft. www.petzl.com

Photo © www.kalice.fr

Petzl Access the inaccessible®

SISU Shot

Sisu /sē-soo/ - a Finnish word that cannot be translated properly into the English language, loosely translated to mean stoic determination, bravery, resilience, perseverance and hardiness. A trait common with Midwest climbers.

ABOUT THE SHOT:
SOME DAYS DON'T GIVE YOU AN INCH AND YOU HAVE TO EARN EVERY MILE. MUNISING LOCAL MARIO MOLIN KNOWS THIS BETTER THAN ANYONE
: BILL THOMPSON